EMPTY

EMPTY

A Story of Anorexia

Christie Pettit

Revell
Grand Rapids, Michigan

© 2003, 2006 by Christie Pettit

Published by Fleming H. Revell
a division of Baker Publishing Group
P.O. Box 6287, Grand Rapids, MI 49516-6287
www.revellbooks.com

Revised edition of *Starving: A Personal Journey through Anorexia* (© 2003)

Second printing, July 2006

Printed in the United States of America

Library of Congress Cataloging-in-Publication Data
Pettit, Christie.
 Empty : a story of anorexia / Christie Pettit.—Rev. ed.
  p. cm.
 Rev. ed. of: Starving.
 Includes bibliographical references (p.   ).
 ISBN 10: 0-8007-3135-2 (pbk.)
 ISBN 978-0-8007-3135-9 (pbk.)
 1. Pettit, Christie. 2. Anorexia nervosa—Patients—United States—
Biography. I. Pettit, Christie. Starving. II. Title.
 RC552.A5P465 2006
 362.196'852620092—dc22   2006001113

Scripture is taken from the HOLY BIBLE, NEW INTERNATIONAL VERSION®. NIV®. Copyright © 1973, 1978, 1984 by International Bible Society. Used by permission of Zondervan. All rights reserved.

"All in all, when I am at my worst and most controlled by food and exercise, nothing seems to be 'enough.'"

Kate

To all those who have shared their stories with me and all those who struggle silently.

May we all begin to see ourselves as God sees us.

Contents

Part 5 Where Do I Go from Here?

Part 6 Who Am I?

Why I Wrote This Book

Since I began work on this book, many people have asked me why I was writing it. For myself? For other sufferers? For their families? For God? Honestly, I am not sure exactly what has motivated me to tell my story. Each of these reasons has driven me at one time or another. Ultimately, I feel I have no other choice but to tell my story—for myself, for others, and for God.

I suppose I write because I am looking for answers. I have so many questions about my experience with anorexia. Why did this happen to me? What made it happen? How did I become so self-absorbed? What do I share with others? What does my experience, and the experience of so many other young women, mean for our society? How do I reconstruct my self-image after such an ordeal? How did this experience contribute to the person I am now? Where do I go from here?

My research has brought me in contact with the stories of many who have had similar experiences. One meaningful book I read was Marya Hornbacher's autobiography, *Wasted: A Memoir of Anorexia and Bulimia.* Her words motivated me to write, to reach people as she had reached me. In the opening chapter, she writes, "I would do anything to keep people from going where I went. Writing this book was the only thing I could think of" (7). When her story touched my heart, I thought that perhaps sharing my story could do the same for someone else. I too felt the overwhelming urge to share, to express, to explain, to try to understand.

But my motivation to write doesn't come only from my concerns about eating disorders. Although I do wish to learn more about eating disorders and their complex impact on our society, I also want to focus on the deeper spiritual level of my experiences. More than anything else, my battle with my body has been an intense spiritual journey. I feel compelled to share what I have learned about God along the way.

Roberta C. Bondi, professor of theology at Emory University, writes about how she discovered the benefit of sharing her personal spiritual experiences. She writes, "For me, it was only as I was able to tell these stories of my own life to God that I was even able to hear for myself what it was I needed to ask God for, to ask for it, and to receive it" (13). Although my struggle with anorexia has been the most difficult thing I have ever been through, the spiritual journey through this time in my life has been priceless. Like Roberta Bondi, I want to write my story, to share my life as an act of gratitude for God's presence with me throughout this experience.

In the introduction to his autobiography about his involvement in the Watergate scandal, Charles Colson writes, "I have been given a tremendous eagerness to share all this with others. As you travel with me through these pages, my hope is that you will ask for God's hand in your life" (12). I know that my struggle has revealed great lessons to me. As I write, each layer of the mystery of this experience seems to be peeled away. I long to uncover the mysteries of eating disorders and also to help others travel closer to God just as I have. Just as Colson wrote to make sense out of his experiences, I also now attempt to tell my story.

Obviously a lot of things are motivating me to write about my experiences as an anorexic Christian. Each time I sit down to write, it seems to be for a different reason. Regardless of the mysterious ways that God has brought me to write this book and you to read it, I invite you to embark with me on a journey through the spirit and mind of someone who has been plagued by anorexia.

It is my sincere hope that reading my story will help others better understand their own life stories, but it should be noted that my writing is not intended to replace the benefit of professional counseling. It is also my personal story. Your experience or the experience of someone you love who is struggling with anorexia will be different. Please use this only as one of many tools for healing. If you or someone you love is struggling with an eating disorder, I strongly urge you to seek professional guidance to begin the recovery process.

I would also like to note that although this discussion of anorexia is told from a feminine perspective, this disorder affects not only women but also men. I have chosen to focus on the specifically female experience of this disorder because of the role being a young woman played in my own struggles.

This Is My Story

I would like to share my story with you. This is a story of struggle, of heartache, of loneliness, of love, and of growth. This is the story of my battle with my body during my freshman year of college. I want to tell you this story because I think there might be something in it that you can relate to—whether from your own experiences or from watching a friend or family member struggle with the same issues.

Eating disorders have become frighteningly common in our country today. On the spectrum from healthy habits to full-blown eating disorders, too many teens are controlled by their exercise routine or eating habits in ways that are limiting the fullness of their lives. Maybe you're one of them. Even if you don't struggle with one of the more severe disorders, you may struggle with your appearance and your identity in some respect or another. Most of us feel fat, unattractive, awkward, lost, insecure, pressured to perform, out of control, or plain uncomfortable in our own skin at some point. Many of these feelings are a normal part of development, but your life doesn't have to be dominated by them.

I hope that by reading some of the details from a time in my life when I was consumed by these issues, you'll be encouraged to break free from your own bondage. It wasn't until my life began to spin out of control that I realized that things could be different. My life didn't have to be about how much I had exercised or how disciplined I had been with my diet. I found hope that life could be more, much more.

Part of the reason my struggles progressed into an eating disorder was the misconception I had about what it meant to have an eating disorder. I thought that people who were anorexic never ate and then looked in the mirror and thought they were fat when they were actually thin. Although these may be *some* symptoms of an eating disorder, different people can struggle in this area in a lot of different ways. As a college athlete, my focus was much more on performance and overexercising than it was on how I looked. My goal was to be at my ideal weight so that I could be the best tennis player that I could be. I ate three meals a day and a snack before practice, so I never thought that I was anorexic.

The problem was in how strict I became about what I ate and in how obsessive I became about exercising. I believe that if I had been more aware of these symptoms and if I had had a better understanding of what it meant to have an eating disorder or to be a compulsive exerciser, I would not have let these habits begin to control my life so much. That's why I want to broaden your understanding of eating disorders and help you to recognize unhealthy behavior before it becomes worse. The earlier that symptoms are identified, the easier it is to change unhealthy habits.

At first glance you might think this is a book about the importance of healthy eating. But that's actually not the main thing I want you to hear. The eating and weight issues that I talk about here are an external sign of a deeper struggle, one that we all wrestle with. The theme of this book is identity development—the journey of discovering who you are. We all long to feel special, and the truth is that we are indeed each unique. The story of my eating disorder is really about a time in my life when I was trying to figure out who I was and who I wanted to be.

As you read this story, I invite you to think about your own story. What has your relationship with food, exercise, and your body been like so far in life? How would you like for it to be different? Who do you want to be? What's important to you? Develop your own story and share it with others. You will not only understand yourself better but also impact others by what you say and who you are.

To help you better understand your own story, I have included comments I have heard from other young women who have also struggled with these issues. Their comments show different aspects of the struggles we all have with our bodies, food, and exercise. The names are fictitious and some of the details have been changed to protect those who have so openly shared their experiences with me. But I've included their quotes because I want to challenge you to think about how *you* might express your own feelings about these issues. Every person's relationship with their body is different, so I hope these other perspectives help you think about your own story. Your story is unique—but I believe that as you think about what parts of my story and their stories you can relate to, you will begin to know yourself better.

It's a blessing to be able to share my story with you . . .

When I was eighteen, I left my home in Houston, Texas, to attend the University of Virginia on a tennis scholarship. I knew almost nothing about eating disorders. I had heard that they were prevalent among female college athletes, but I certainly never considered myself a candidate. I was strong and healthy, a fit athlete who had never been concerned with weight.

Like most college freshmen, in the first couple of months I gained some weight. I didn't like the idea of gaining the "freshman fifteen," so in mid-October I decided I would be more careful about what I ate and start doing some extra cardiovascular exercise. Although my tennis workouts were fairly strenuous, they didn't involve any long-distance running or biking. I thought this might be good for me. I knew that being in better shape would help me as a player.

At first I decided I wouldn't have the desserts offered at the dining hall each day. Then I chose healthier meals as well. Over time I found myself having a salad for dinner every night. At every meal I ate the healthiest thing I could find. The athletic dining hall had better food choices than most college dining halls, with many healthy options and clearly marked nutrition labels. This only encouraged my newfound quest for health. I allowed myself few indulgences, staying on a strict diet.

Society teaches girls that they should always be in the diet mentality. As a result of the diet craze in our country, I didn't think my behavior was abnormal. I ate lots of vegetables and fruits and other things I had always been taught were good for me. I thought I was finally taking care of myself.

Eventually, however, my anxiety about my weight increased, and I stopped going to the dining hall altogether. I became afraid of food. I felt like I always ate too much, and there was so much "bad" food at the dining hall that I couldn't trust myself to stay on my diet if I went there. I labeled cakes and fried foods as forbidden, but eventually I even thought that meat was a waste of calories. The more I worked out, the more I restricted my diet. It was easy to convince myself that certain foods weren't worth the extra time I'd need to spend exercising to burn off the calories.

Throughout this time it never occurred to me that I had an eating disorder. I lost weight continuously over the year, but I always thought I would level off at my ideal body weight. Since I had never dieted before, I didn't know what my leanest body weight was. Unfortunately, I just kept losing weight.

When I came home from school at the end of my first year, many people expressed concern. Just to prove to everyone (and myself) that I was all right, I went in for a checkup. My doctor said I was healthy but that I certainly had lost a considerable amount of weight. In fact, I had lost about twenty-five pounds from October until May. He told me about anorexia, but I still did not think that was what was wrong with me. After my examination, my doctor and I decided that as long as I didn't lose any more weight over the summer, I would be fine.

It was a nice goal, but unfortunately, it didn't happen.

That summer I taught tennis. This extra activity, combined with my daily workouts and tennis practice, was too much for my body to handle. By the end of the summer I had lost another five pounds. I had lost a total of thirty pounds and was at my lowest weight. When I returned to school my coach was worried. Following NCAA regulations, he sent me to have a checkup at student health services and to see a counselor and a nutritionist. The doctor said I had an unusually slow heartbeat and that I needed to cut back on my exercise. The counselor said I was anorexic and that I should come in weekly to work through my problems. My nutritionist gave me an outline of what my diet should be.

All of this was so overwhelming. I began to see how serious my problem was. That fall I met with a counselor regularly and learned a lot about what had been going on in my head. By the next semester my counselor and I decided I didn't need to come in anymore, but I continued to work on my recovery on my own. Over the school year I gained about eight pounds and made considerable strides toward recovery. This period of battling back from anorexia was the most challenging time of my life.

I have kept a journal regularly since high school. As a result, I recorded many of my thoughts throughout the development of my eating disorder. These entries show how my attempt to lose a few pounds grew into a clinically diagnosed case of anorexia. My hope is that sharing my story will help others to better understand what it is like to suffer from an eating disorder.

Is Something Wrong with Me?

I see now that the first part of my journey through anorexia addresses the issue of determining whether or not something was wrong with me. I was beginning to have the sense that I was not myself, but I wasn't sure what was really going on in my life. Each part of my story looks at a different question that I was wrestling with as I was trying to understand what was happening to me. The first step on my road to recovery was to recognize that there was indeed a problem. This is often the most difficult step to take. It can be quite a challenge for someone who is struggling with food or exercise issues to acknowledge that there is a problem that needs to be addressed. These opening journal entries reflect the time in my life when I was asking myself the question, Is something wrong with me?

The Beginning

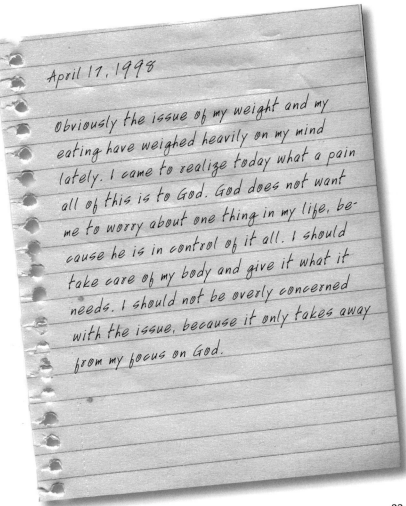

April 17, 1998

Obviously the issue of my weight and my eating have weighed heavily on my mind lately. I came to realize today what a pain all of this is to God. God does not want me to worry about one thing in my life, because he is in control of it all. I should take care of my body and give it what it needs. I should not be overly concerned with the issue, because it only takes away from my focus on God.

I set out to lose some weight in mid-October, but the first time I mentioned it as a concern in my journal was in mid-April. It never occurred to me that I might be developing an eating disorder. I didn't have any of the classic symptoms. I never looked at myself in the mirror and saw myself as fat when I was not. I never felt like I was making myself go hungry, although I later came to realize I had just become numb to signs of hunger. In my mind, people who had eating disorders had severe emotional problems. I had always been happy and well-adjusted. I was not trying to harm myself. I was simply trying to take exceptional care of myself, to be as healthy as I could be.

In the beginning, I simply made healthy changes to my diet: more fruit and fewer potato chips. Even with these changes, I always felt I had the energy to do what I needed to do in my tennis practices and all my other activities. In fact, at first my body enjoyed the healthy changes to my diet. It was not until the summer after my first year in college that all my efforts to be

"When I was most focused on working out, I felt like it was my first and last thought of every day. I had to know exactly when and where I was going to work out and, furthermore, exactly the time. I preferred to do it first thing in the morning—that way I was certain to get it in, and I also felt like I could do more at that hour since it was the start of the day."—Elizabeth

"Once when I was nine years old, my mom came into my room, where I was reading, and asked if I wanted to go outside and play. Although this was a seemingly innocent question, what I thought when she said this was, 'Mom said I should go out and play. She doesn't want me to just sit here and be inactive.' I glanced down and noticed my inactive body and concluded, 'Mom thinks I'm fat and wants me to go outside and be active so I won't be fat anymore.'"—Susan

"I started losing weight because I was somewhere new, somewhere unfamiliar, and in desperate need of having an identity. Exercise was so easy when I was feeling so bad about the rest of my life. I could feel good and be in complete and total control."—Catherine

Is Something Wrong with Me?

healthy—my vigorous exercise and restricted diet—really started to take a toll on my body.

My relationship with God is the center of my life. I became a Christian during my junior year in high school, and ever since then my faith has been my focal point. It was not until I realized that being overly concerned with my weight was sinful in God's eyes that I became aware that something was wrong in my life. I realized that my attitude toward my weight was not what God wanted from me. Mark 7:8 says, "You have let go of the commands of God and are holding on to the traditions of men." As much as I didn't want to admit it to myself, over the past few months I had gradually been replacing what I knew to be true about myself as a Christian with the world's standards about beauty and appearance.

I realized something was wrong because thoughts about food and working out consumed me throughout each day. I was constantly planning when I was going to fit in exercise and how I was going to eat the healthiest meal. I had also begun to calculate the smallest amount of food I could eat and still have the energy to do what I wanted to do. Even in the early stages of my problem I could see that I was becoming obsessed, and it was starting to take over my life.

Frustration

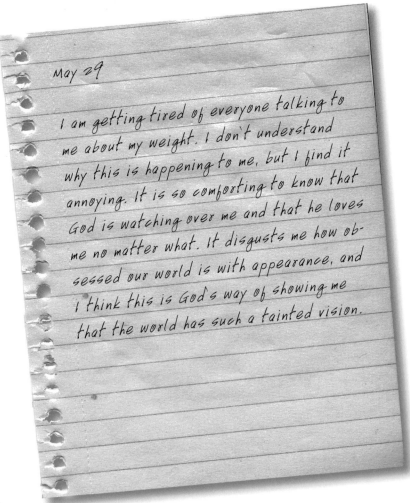

May 29

I am getting tired of everyone talking to me about my weight. I don't understand why this is happening to me, but I find it annoying. It is so comforting to know that God is watching over me and that he loves me no matter what. It disgusts me how obsessed our world is with appearance, and I think this is God's way of showing me that the world has such a tainted vision.

I remember getting extraordinarily frustrated because so many people were confronting me about my weight. I felt like everyone was talking about me behind my back and judging what I did or didn't eat. It's clear to me now that these people were only acting out of concern for my well-being, but when I didn't want to admit I had a problem, I confused their concern with personal attack.

In the beginning of my weight loss, I was frustrated that I was labeled (especially by those who didn't know me well) as having an eating disorder. At the University of Virginia it seemed like any girl who was careful about her weight and exercised on a regular basis was suspected of having a problem. I got angry because I didn't appreciate being categorized like that, but in reality I was just afraid it was true. It was people's comments and concerns, however, that eventually encouraged me to take a serious look at what I was doing to myself.

"I think that if I lose all my weight I'll be the real me and I'll be so happy and have no problems. I think people and boys will like me more. I often feel ashamed of my body and embarrassed of my weight and sometimes height."—Dawn

"I feel like my body will never, never be the way I want it to be and like it's just ugly. I feel self-conscious and ashamed."—Jen

Frustration

Knowing how to approach someone you think might have an eating disorder is hard, but as long as you act out of love, I don't think there is a wrong approach. The most important thing is to communicate unconditional love and support. It is also helpful to have specific examples about their behavior. For instance, if you can give examples of times when they were moody, exercised too much, or deliberately avoided food, that can help call attention to behavior which might be a problem. Some things may be better received than others, but in the end the suffering person will feel the love being expressed, no matter what words are chosen. What you say is not as important as how you say it. Also remember that although your concern may not be well received at the time, that doesn't mean you haven't made an impression that could lead to change.

When I first lost weight many people commented to me about how good they thought I looked. It made me feel good that I had dropped the extra pounds. I enjoyed the compliments. I had never considered myself to be an extraordinarily attractive girl, so I enjoyed having so many people comment on my appearance. I also felt more noticed by guys. In March the guy of my dreams asked me out for the first time, which only fed my desire to be thin and feel beautiful.

Unfortunately, I fell into the dangerous trap addressed in the book of 1 Peter. I was basing my opinion of myself on my external appearance rather than on my inner self. "Your beauty should not come from outward adornment, such as braided hair and the wearing of gold jewelry and fine clothes. Instead, it should be that of your inner self, the unfading beauty of a gentle and quiet spirit, which is of great worth in God's sight" (1 Peter 3:3–4). Receiving praise for my outward appearance made me focus on my external rather than my internal self-worth. I was tested by my pride and the praise I received for my weight loss, and it got the best of me.

Just when I was becoming dependent on these compliments, however, the flattering remarks quickly turned to concern. I couldn't believe how rapidly people's opinions could change. I was confused because I had equated being thin with being beautiful, but this no longer seemed to be the case. I enjoyed the positive attention, but the negative judgments bothered me. I didn't like the idea of anyone thinking I had any sort of problem. I did not want to see my problem, and I certainly didn't want anyone else to know about it. The more people expressed concern, the more I wanted them to leave me alone.

Denial

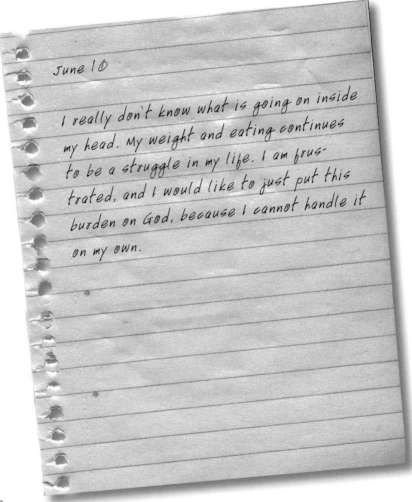

June 10

I really don't know what is going on inside my head. My weight and eating continues to be a struggle in my life. I am frustrated, and I would like to just put this burden on God, because I cannot handle it on my own.

My first attempt to deal with my problem was to seek God's help. I recognized that what was going on in my thoughts was more than I could deal with on my own, but I wasn't sure what to do. I didn't want to face the fact that I had a problem. It was easier to generalize my frustration and ask God to help me. I wasn't ready to look at what I was doing to myself, so I couldn't even understand what I needed help with.

Until this time in my life, I had been fairly carefree. I was happy, and it seemed like everything in my life was going great. In my mind, my first year of college had been the best year of my life. I had made great friends and done well both in tennis and in school. I had a new boyfriend I really liked. On the surface everything seemed to be going my way. I thought if I could just stop thinking so much about my weight, everything would be perfect. Unfortunately, things were not that simple. This journal entry reflects the fact that in my heart I knew something was not right.

"I lied a lot of the time to try to cover up for what was a very distorted and wrong way of thinking."—Eden

Denial

Signs of Negative Body Image

1. You are unable to accept a compliment.
2. Your mood is affected by how you think you look.
3. Constantly comparing yourself to others.
4. Calling yourself disparaging names—fat, gross, ugly, flabby.
5. Attempting to create a "perfect" image.
6. Seeking constant reassurance from others that your looks are acceptable.
7. Consistently overestimating the size of your body or body parts.
8. Believing that if you could attain your goal weight or size, you would accept yourself.
9. Allowing the drive for thinness to be more important than all of life's pleasures or goals.
10. Equating thinness with beauty, success, perfection, happiness, confidence, and self-control.
11. Thinking of the body as separate parts (thighs, stomach, buttocks, hips, etc.) rather than feeling connected to the whole body.
12. Having an ever-present fear of being fat—even if you are slim.
13. Being controlled by a strong sense of shame about yourself and your body.

Adapted from the Renfrew Center, www.renfrewcenter.com

Irritability

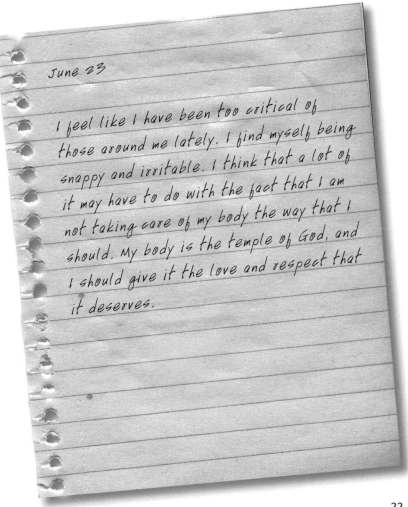

June 23

I feel like I have been too critical of those around me lately. I find myself being snappy and irritable. I think that a lot of it may have to do with the fact that I am not taking care of my body the way that I should. My body is the temple of God, and I should give it the love and respect that it deserves.

By now my body was beginning to cry out for help. I not only was strict with the amount of calories I consumed each day but also had completely depleted my body of any reserves it had stored. Because I didn't allow myself to eat enough during the day, I was irritable, especially in the late afternoon. I had ignored my body's signals for so long that I could no longer recognize hunger, but I convinced myself that I was eating plenty. I often felt weak, and this affected my moods.

Not only was I not eating enough, I also had myself on a rigorous workout routine. Every day I would push myself in my workouts until I felt like I had nothing left. I woke up at 6:00 a.m. every morning and went running until I couldn't run any longer. Then I would work all day teaching tennis, squeezing in my own practice during lunch. I now understand why I would be almost too tired to function throughout an entire day, but at the time I thought I should be

"My mood became affected by when and how much exercise I was getting. I was having a good day if I got to work out. I was in a significantly better mood if I worked out in the morning as opposed to waiting until later in the day."—Laura

"Everyday things that should be fun—like going out to eat with friends—take on a whole new meaning. It is a time that is uncomfortable and frustrating. I get grouchy for not being able to eat what I want."—Katrina

"When I do indulge, I get angry with myself and just am depressed about it. Then that carries over into my general attitude toward others—especially with my boyfriend. I feel completely embarrassed of my body and find it hard to believe him when he might tell me I am beautiful."—Brenda

"When I was really struggling with these issues, I felt consistently anxious and never at rest in my soul. I woke up thinking about food and spent most of my energy exercising (running at least six miles a day) and worrying about what and when I would eat. It consumed me and began to change my personality and stole the joy and excitement away from living. I found myself wondering, Will this ever stop?"—Ella

able to do anything. I ignored my body telling me I was tired just as I ignored my body telling me I was hungry.

Despite these warning signs, I still thought I was just an athlete in training. After all, eating healthy and exercising were supposed to be good for me. I have always been a perfectionist, and I was taking my fitness to the extreme. I placed absurd demands on my body and pushed myself to my breaking point every day.

During this summer I started to see how my eating disorder was interfering with the rest of my life. Because I spent so much time and energy on my fitness, I was incapable of functioning in normal daily life. My irritability and moodiness were a noticeable problem.

My moods indicated to me that I was not treating myself well. First Corinthians 6:19–20 says, "Do you not know that your body is a temple of the Holy Spirit, who is in you, whom you have received from God? You are not your own; you were bought at a price. Therefore honor God with your body." I knew in my heart that I wasn't honoring God with my body. I was punishing my body daily with a lack of food and too much exercise—hardly nurturing myself as God's temple.

Diet Distortions

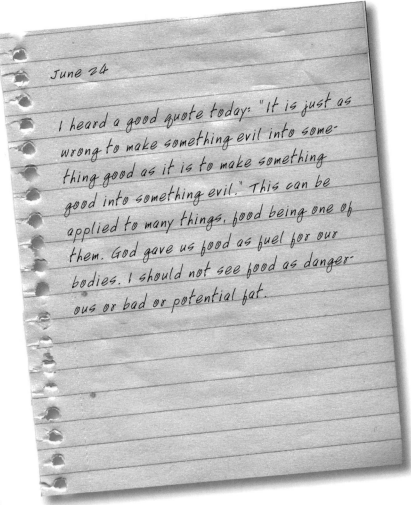

June 24

I heard a good quote today: "It is just as wrong to make something evil into something good as it is to make something good into something evil." This can be applied to many things, food being one of them. God gave us food as fuel for our bodies. I should not see food as dangerous or bad or potential fat.

This entry reveals how distorted my views about food actually were. God gave us food as a source of energy and a pleasure to be enjoyed, but I had taught myself to look at food as potential fat on my body. With all the nonfat foods available, I could make it through an entire day eating virtually no fat. Unfortunately, this makes for an unhealthy diet. But I always felt that if I didn't choose the non-fat alternative, I wasn't being as healthy as I could be. I labeled foods that contained fat as "bad" for me. I made strict rules for myself about food, and I stuck to them religiously.

This type of thinking, referred to as the "diet mentality," came from social pressure. Dieting is everywhere in our country today. Joan Jacobs Brumberg (*Fasting Girls*, 250) reported that close to 80 percent of preteen girls, some even as young as eight or nine, watch what they eat because they don't want to get fat. I thought girls who were skinny always ordered nonfat salad

"Sometimes eating is an enemy—I overthink about food. I would love to accept myself and food regardless of what I look like."—Kara

"I love food! And I think that is really bad."—Betsy

"In the past, food was my enemy. I used to exercise to get rid of the damage I had done by overeating. I realized a few years ago that I had a problem that had been building since an early age. But by this point I had a severe problem with overeating to achieve the 'numb' feeling to escape problems. I knew it was really bad when I started working out hard afterward and taking laxatives. Food became my idol. My day revolved around planning my next meal as I tried to control it."—Misty

dressing on the side and no cheese or eggs or bacon. When my friends and I went out to dinner, most of the girls ordered this way, but the problem was that I did it all the time.

My labeling foods as "bad" began with simple things like chips and fried foods, but it snowballed into something dangerous. I started with basic "no-no's" like fatty desserts, but eventually there were more foods I could live without or viewed as a waste of calories. I convinced myself that things like pasta and meat would make me bulk up. My judgments about which foods were good for me and which foods were not had become quite distorted.

I was constantly trying to find ways to eat the most food with the fewest calories. All day I counted the calories I consumed. I was always aware of how many calories were in whatever I was eating. I judged the amount of food I needed to eat based on how many calories I would allow myself rather than on whether my body told me I was hungry. I had heard of anorexic girls who barely let themselves eat, and I was still eating at least three meals a day. So I thought I was fine. I just wasn't letting myself eat quite enough day after day.

As part of my recovery, I have read extensively about this diet mentality. The term *diet mentality* refers to being extraordinarily careful about what you eat and always trying to control how much you consume rather than letting your body tell you when to start and when to stop eating. Many women, like myself, feel they must constantly live in this kind of diet mentality, always monitoring how much they consume. The diet mentality and the concept of calorie counting began as early as the 1920s, and it has had devastating effects on women ever since. As Brumberg wrote, "With the popularization of the concept of calorie counting, physical features once regarded as natural—such as appetite and body weight—were designated as objects of conscious control" (*Fasting Girls*, 240). How could this possibly be how God intended us to think about food? The diet mentality is extremely unnatural. God meant for food to be enjoyed and to be used as fuel.

The Breaking Point

July 13

I feel completely and utterly broken. I am so tired of dealing with this weight issue, and I don't know what to do. I am utterly alone and sad. I can't handle this by myself. I thought I could, but I can't. "Lord, I come to you weak and defeated. Please help me with this burden that you have put on my shoulders. Free me from this sin. Take me into your loving arms and comfort me." I hate what this obsession is doing to me. I hate who I have become, and yet I am not willing to give it up. My physical weight is not the problem here. The problem is what is going on inside my head. I know that God is in control. He will teach me a lot through this trial, but right now I am at my weakest point. I feel so very, very low.

This was the first time I admitted to myself that I had become obsessed. I remember sitting in my room alone at night and breaking into tears. It was as if I had suddenly woken up and realized that I was self-destructing. It was horrible to have to face what I had let happen to me. I didn't know how I had gotten to that point or how to make it go away. I felt completely unequipped to deal with what was going on inside my head. By now it seemed as if food and my weight were all I ever thought about. I was terrified of being fat, and yet I knew I was too skinny. I loved being too skinny. As I wrote here, "My physical weight is not the problem." I was dangerously underweight, but I simply loved it.

If I did not kill myself with my workouts every day, I feared getting fat. If I ate too much, I feared getting fat. I spent the majority of each day planning what I would eat next. I knew my thoughts shouldn't be so consumed with food, but I didn't

"I feel fat, gross, disgusting. No matter what I do, I will always be that way. Even if I starve and work out all the time, I will never look how I want to. I have never been happy with what I see in the mirror."—Holly

"I didn't eat for two days one time, because I thought the only way to be a better runner was to lose weight and that starving myself was the only way."—Nicole

"I was never anorexic, I had just lost a lot of weight incredibly fast, and people were beginning to take note, fast. I had never been the 'thin' girl before. I was always athletic, someone who was comfortable in her own skin, enjoyed having others around at all times, and was pretty easygoing. I was a lot of fun. In those days when I was thinner than normal, I was miserable. I felt like I was living in chains."—Jenny

know how to change these horrible habits I had developed. I was petrified of what I had done to myself.

In this entry I described the loneliness I felt. *Any kind of obsession can seriously isolate a person.* I felt like no one could really understand what I was experiencing. After all, *I* did not even understand what I was thinking, so how could anyone else? Everyone seemed to have an opinion about what was going on with me, and that made me defensive. In addition, most people were concerned but didn't know what to say or how to say it. So they just avoided me and avoided the issue altogether. I have never felt so alone.

Food is an important part of social interaction. Because I was obsessed with what I ate, I was uncomfortable going out to dinner or being around people while they were eating. My obsession made others feel awkward about eating with me as well. My friends and family no longer enjoyed sharing meals with me. Who wants to have dinner with someone who anxiously picks at food all night or always orders a salad? I was much more comfortable eating alone anyway. Only alone could I exert total control over what I ate. This pattern of behavior is a lot like an alcoholic drinking alone and should therefore be considered a similar warning sign.

I wanted to be in control of my food. As a result, I would fight with my mom whenever she tried to fix me dinner. I claimed that I was trying to learn how to cook, but I really just wanted to have complete control over how the food was prepared and what was in it. All of these factors combined to leave me feeling extremely isolated, especially from the people who were closest to me.

At this point in my life I knew I could not cure myself of my obsession on my own, but I still wasn't ready to get professional help. I still didn't truly believe I was anorexic. I thought I just needed to straighten out the confused thoughts in my head. I certainly never thought my body was in any real danger. I thought I would be able to recover through prayer and some serious soul-searching. I thought that with God's help my problem would just go away. Unfortunately, I didn't know how severe my problem was. My denial proved to be extremely destructive. It only lengthened the amount of time I battled anorexia and allowed it to affect more areas of my life.

For example, my feelings of loneliness had begun to infect my spiritual life. I not only felt isolated from my friends and family, but I also felt I was letting God down. After all, doesn't the Bible promise that we can do all things through Christ? So if I couldn't pray this away, what was wrong with my faith? I thought that if I would only concentrate harder when I prayed or pray more wholeheartedly, then God would heal me. I have since realized that God was with me through this time, just as he is always with me. I was not alone, but I needed to work through my problem so I could learn from all that he was trying to teach me.

Running from the Problem

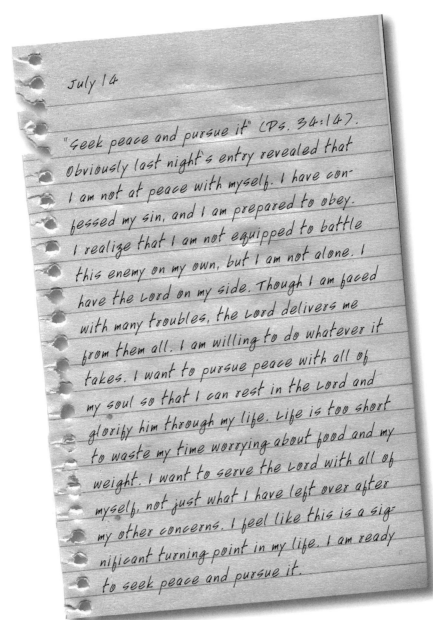

July 14

"Seek peace and pursue it" (Ps. 34:14). Obviously last night's entry revealed that I am not at peace with myself. I have confessed my sin, and I am prepared to obey. I realize that I am not equipped to battle this enemy on my own, but I am not alone. I have the Lord on my side. Though I am faced with many troubles, the Lord delivers me from them all. I am willing to do whatever it takes. I want to pursue peace with all of my soul so that I can rest in the Lord and glorify him through my life. Life is too short to waste my time worrying about food and my weight. I want to serve the Lord with all of myself, not just what I have left over after my other concerns. I feel like this is a significant turning point in my life. I am ready to seek peace and pursue it.

I included this entry not because of the truth of what I said but because it shows how desperately I wanted to escape from the reality of my anorexia. I wanted to wake up the morning after my breaking point and start afresh—to turn a new leaf and instantly get my life back on track. Having an eating disorder is like being on a roller coaster. One minute you feel completely down, as I did the night before. The next minute you have a new resolve to fight. Unfortunately, I had no idea how many similar ups and downs I would go through as I struggled to regain my life. At this point I finally knew I had a problem. I also knew in my heart that I really wanted to get better. When I awoke ready to be freed from my obsession, I thought the worst of things was over. I thought if I set my mind to it and I prayed, everything would be all right.

Although I recognized that I had some sort of problem, I still was not sure what exactly was wrong with me. Unfortunately,

"These struggles have made me see how much I need God. It is so hard to overcome something that haunts you day in and day out. Without faith and without some sort of greater purpose, it's hard to see past yourself."—Frances

my issues were much more severe than I suspected. I had been developing bad habits for about nine months, and by now they were ingrained in my life. Any habit is hard to change, and I didn't realize how deeply I had wounded myself. Recovery would be much more difficult than I could have ever imagined.

Although denial is one of the biggest hurdles victims of eating disorders must overcome, I believe that the reason I was so quickly able to recognize that things were not right in my life was because of my spiritual life. My reflection time with God made me look truthfully at myself and helped me to see what had developed into a serious issue. If I hadn't had my faith, I'm not sure I would have ever faced up to my eating disorder and admitted that I was obsessed.

Although my relationship with God ultimately gave me the strength to overcome my eating disorder, my faith also was a problem for me in a way. I found it extremely difficult to ask others for help with my eating disorder because I thought I should be able to work it out with God's help. I thought if I simply prayed for God to free me from my obsession, I would be normal again. I have since learned that there is nothing wrong with getting help from others and that God actually gives us other people so that we can strengthen one another. Proverbs tells us, "As iron sharpens iron, so one man sharpens another" (27:17). There are times in our lives when we need the support of others, when we must admit that we cannot survive on our own. God gives us other people so that we can help each other, encourage each other, and work together for his kingdom.

I regret that I put off getting help for so long. I expected to be able to heal myself through prayer alone. I read verses such as Mark 11:24—"Therefore I tell you, whatever you ask for in prayer, believe that you have received it, and it will be yours"—and I took them to mean that if I only prayed harder, if I only believed more deeply, then God would simply take my problem away. I am not at all trying to question the effects of prayer, but I was not equipped to handle the severity of my problem on my own. I had to have some outside help and support. I believe that in the end, however, my prayers and my relationship with God ultimately gave me the strength to recover. My prayers motivated me to seek help and gave me the strength to fight for my life.

What Is Really Going On?

After beginning to admit that I did have issues regarding food and exercise that were controlling me, the next step in the process of recovery involved more fully identifying what the problem was. Self-awareness is an important part of health and wholeness. Although I am a fairly self-reflective person, I had been clueless about how serious my problem was as it developed during my first year in college. This next step of starting to identify the self-destructive behaviors and thought patterns that I had developed was an important part of growing in my self-awareness. In these next journal entries I am asking myself the question, What is really going on?

Judging Others

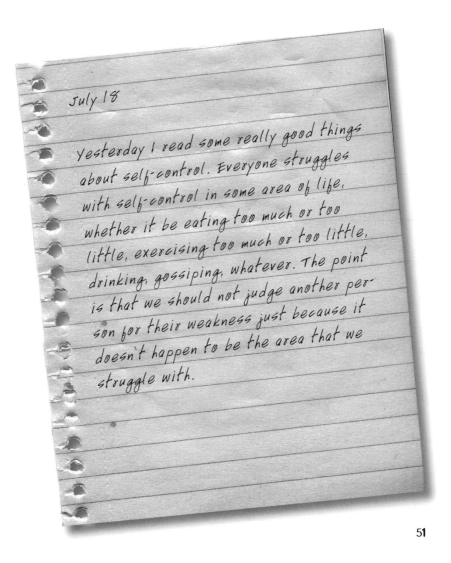

July 18

Yesterday I read some really good things about self-control. Everyone struggles with self-control in some area of life, whether it be eating too much or too little, exercising too much or too little, drinking, gossiping, whatever. The point is that we should not judge another person for their weakness just because it doesn't happen to be the area that we struggle with.

This entry shows how I struggled with judging other people. I was uncomfortable being around people who were overweight (in my eyes), especially while they were eating. I couldn't understand why they couldn't show more self-control. I thought everyone should live with the same diet mentality I had. It made me angry to see other people indulge, because I wouldn't allow myself to indulge. I couldn't understand why I had to be so strict with myself when others could eat whatever they wanted.

My judgmental attitude is another good example of how my obsession interfered with my relationships. I got irritated with people for the way they ate. I judged them in terms of their weight and as a result lost all sensible perspective of others. The tension my eating disorder caused between me and the people I love eventually motivated me to get better. My family has always been close, and I hated the distance I felt from my mom, my dad, and my brother as a result of my anorexia. In addition, as I was falling in love with Peter ("the guy

"People (especially guys) will like me more if I stay fit and look pretty. Girls will be more willing to accept me if I wear the right clothes and have a good tan."—Samantha

"I recall one time when my mother was trying to understand how I thought about weight, food, and body types. She is not a large woman at all. But one time she asked, 'Do you think I am fat?' I replied, 'No,' but in my head I was thinking, 'Yes, of course you're fat. Can't you see that yourself?'"—Kelly

of my dreams" mentioned earlier) that summer, I knew I did not want to do anything to jeopardize that special relationship. It was impossible for me to relate to people normally since I was developing such a skewed perspective on life.

Throughout the Bible God warns us against judging other people. Matthew 7:1–2 says, "Do not judge, or you too will be judged. For in the same way you judge others, you will be judged, and with the measure you use, it will be measured to you." This was exactly my problem. Because I judged my self-worth entirely in terms of my weight, I applied the same standard to everyone else. Any time I came into contact with a person, my first thought was a judgment of their self-control and self-worth based on their body size and shape. When I saw old friends from high school, I judged their first year at college based on how much weight they had gained or lost. I felt a sense of power over my friends who had gained weight, since I decided that I was happier at school because I had lost weight.

Although I judged others harshly, I was even more critical of myself. I constantly evaluated my body on the scale or in front of the mirror. How I felt about myself each day was determined by what I ate and how much I exercised. I would berate myself with guilt if I indulged. Having a full stomach made me feel as if I had done something wrong. If I felt full, I thought that I had stuffed myself unforgivably. When I experienced this guilt, I added extra exercise to my routine to work off what I had eaten. To punish myself for indulging, I would also be strict about what I allowed myself to eat at my next couple of meals. For example, if I ate a big dinner, I would limit my breakfast and lunch the next day. A heavy sense of guilt loomed over most meals.

I had trained myself to feel good if I ate only a little and feel bad if I ate too much. A positive opinion of myself was

An absence of both self-acceptance and self-worth are at the root of eating disorders. I have learned throughout my struggles that I have to be able to love and accept myself if I want to be able to love and accept others. Each day I try to work toward greater self-acceptance. When I talk with other women who have struggled with an eating disorder, this is always the first thing that comes up. Even after counseling and recovery, issues of body image and self-worth linger. This is definitely one of the biggest issues behind eating disorders.

That's why if you are dealing with a victim of an eating disorder, you need to remember that a distorted sense of self-worth is often at the root of her problems. Most likely the victim feels worse about herself than you could imagine. Try to realize this and be sensitive to the tremendous insecurities she is struggling with. **More than anything else, a victim of an eating disorder needs to find a way to have a positive sense of self-worth that doesn't have anything to do with weight and body image.** That is why, the way I see it, a spiritual faith is one of the most important tools in recovery. Defining herself spiritually allows the victim to focus on other aspects of who she is, separate from her outward appearance. Only through serious study of my self-worth as a Christian was I able to tackle the damage my eating disorder had done to my sense of self-worth.

---

completely based on how little I ate and how much I exercised. My self-acceptance was based on my thinness and my ability to show extreme self-control. It has been hard to convince myself that no matter how much I eat, no matter how much I exercise, no matter how much I weigh, I am still the same person. One of the most difficult things for me to learn has been to accept myself unconditionally.

Through the process of recovery, I have realized the danger of basing my worth on things of this world. Many verses proved priceless to me throughout this journey of recovering my sense of self-worth. For example, Ecclesiastes 2:11 says, "Yet when I surveyed all that my hands had done and what I had toiled to achieve, everything was meaningless, a chasing after the wind; nothing was gained under the sun." I realized that a self-worth based on my weight was just like chasing after the wind. My life had to have more substance than that.

Shared Suffering

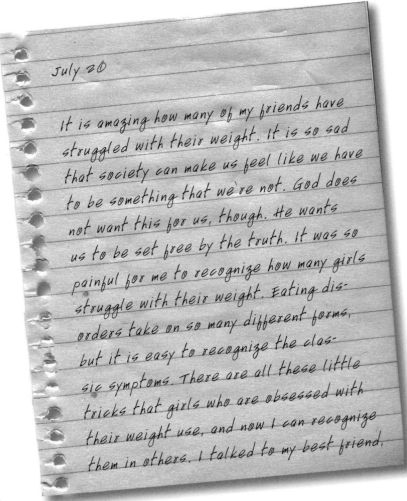

July 20

It is amazing how many of my friends have struggled with their weight. It is so sad that society can make us feel like we have to be something that we're not. God does not want this for us, though. He wants us to be set free by the truth. It was so painful for me to recognize how many girls struggle with their weight. Eating disorders take on so many different forms, but it is easy to recognize the classic symptoms. There are all these little tricks that girls who are obsessed with their weight use, and now I can recognize them in others. I talked to my best friend,

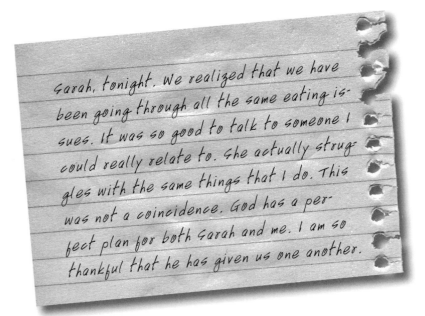

Sarah, tonight. We realized that we have been going through all the same eating issues. It was so good to talk to someone I could really relate to. She actually struggles with the same things that I do. This was not a coincidence. God has a perfect plan for both Sarah and me. I am so thankful that he has given us one another.

As my own experiences opened my eyes to what it meant to have an eating disorder, I was appalled by the number of girls who shared my suffering. Many girls in my high school had battled anorexia right before my eyes, and I had never known it. Now that I've been through it myself, it's easy to recognize girls who have eating disorders. My college campus was covered with them. Out of twelve girls I lived with at school, three had been diagnosed with eating disorders. In addition, four out of the eight girls on my tennis team were anorexic. Almost everyone I knew was concerned with her weight to some extent. Clearly I wasn't alone in my body-conscious mentality.

Once I realized that I had an eating disorder, I suddenly became aware of how many other girls around me shared my struggle. It was as if I had been let into a private club where I knew all the secrets. I could now recognize anyone else who was also a member. I didn't know anything about eating disorders before I went through all this. In high school, two of my best friends had eating disorders, but I was almost oblivious to it. I just thought they didn't eat much. I couldn't truly understand what it was like to have an eating disorder until I went through it myself. Now I knew, and I could recognize when someone else was experiencing it too.

Now that I was more aware of all the signs, I remembered something that had happened earlier in the summer while I was home in Houston. A girl I knew who had recently been in the hospital for an eating disorder reacted very emotionally when she saw me. She aggressively accused me of being anorexic. At the time I had not faced my problem, so I thought she was completely overreacting. Now I can understand why she was so forceful about telling me I was anorexic. Even though I didn't know it yet, she could see right through my façade because she had been through it herself.

"I think what most contributes to my negative body image and emphasis on food and exercise is the people I surround myself with. I feel the absolute worst about myself when I am spending time with someone who is tiny and fit and all they do is talk about how unhappy they are with their body or being so obsessed with exercising and being so concerned with the food they eat. It is impossible to have a healthy perspective on your own body image if you are surrounded by people who have an unhealthy perspective."—Linda

"I have heard that the majority of women struggle with body image, exercise, and eating disorders during high school and college because of being surrounded by a new group of 'competition,' new surroundings, and different situations. I arrived on a school campus to see comparing eyes and competitive spirits. There was definitely an attitude of wanting to be the best, the smartest, the most involved, and definitely the most beautiful, which I suppose these women equated with 'thinness.'"—Annie

Several things can show that someone might have a problem, such as chewing gum all the time and drinking lots of water, coffee, or diet soft drinks. These are ways to avoid eating a lot. Chewing gum tricks your body into thinking it is eating, and drinking lots of water makes your stomach feel full even when it hasn't had enough food. Now when I see someone doing these things, I can also pick up on other habits that are signs, such as avoiding social gatherings that involve food or pretending to be too busy to eat.

The more I developed the skill of recognizing girls who had eating disorders, the more victims I saw. I couldn't believe how many girls had a problem similar to mine. Now it seems as if almost everywhere I go there is someone with whom I share this struggle. I don't know why society makes girls feel like they have to be so skinny, but I know the social pressures have a dangerous effect on today's young women. Pipher writes, "Girls developed eating disorders when our culture developed a standard of beauty that couldn't be obtained by being healthy. When unnatural thinness became attractive, girls did unnatural things to be thin" (184). I think the first solution is increased awareness of the problem. The more people understand what eating disorders are all about, the easier it will be to get help. We need better communication and education.

Cultural values influence self-image. The media tells us that women need to be thin to be attractive. Pipher reports, "In the last two decades we have developed a national cult of thinness. What is considered beautiful has become slimmer and slimmer. For example, in 1950 the White Rock mineral water girl was 5 feet 4 inches tall and weighed 140 pounds. Today she is 5 feet 10 inches and weighs 110 pounds" (184).

Defining Anorexia

A. The individual maintains a body weight that is about 15 percent below normal for age, height, and body type.

B. The individual has an intense fear of gaining weight or becoming fat, even though he or she is underweight. Paradoxically, losing weight can make the fear of gaining even worse.

C. The individual has a distorted body image. Some may feel fat all over; others recognize that they are generally thin but see specific body parts (particularly the stomach and thighs) as being too fat. Self-worth is based on body size and shape. He or she denies that low body weight is a serious cause of concern.

D. In women, there is an absence of at least three consecutive menstrual cycles. A woman also meets this criteria if her period occurs only while she is taking a hormone pill (including, but not limited to, oral contraceptives).

American Psychiatric Association, 544–45

Supermodels today look like skeletons, and it is considered attractive. I definitely received more compliments on my appearance as I began to lose weight.

Although these cultural values seem to influence almost all young women, I don't think it's fair to blame all eating disorders on the media. Our culture creates an environment that increases the problem, but eating disorders are really a sign of a deeper pain. Our culture has provided a way to avoid pain by hiding behind appearance, but the pain still exists.

At this point in my struggle it was comforting for me to know I wasn't alone in my battle. Having a close friend who could relate to my thoughts and feelings eased my loneliness. People who suffer from any sort of addiction often feel alone, so an important part of my healing process was to have friends I could share with. It helped me so much to receive encouragement and support from friends who had been where I was.

However, women who share a common eating disorder often find it hard to relate to one another. *Eating disorders are largely about competition and comparison to others.* I am a competitive person. During my worst times I would thrive on being the girl who ate the least and the healthiest. I had to be the skinniest girl in the room in order to not feel fat. As a result, being around another girl who was also anorexic was very difficult. It became increasingly difficult as I began to recover and gain weight, especially if she was thinner than I was or ate less than I did. I would get jealous that she could continue in the destructive habits and receive the satisfaction of a restrictive diet. I wondered why I had to face my problem if she didn't. It was easier to deny my problem and live in the fantasy of my obsession than it was to start facing it. All these factors made the beginning of my recovery a tense time to be around friends who also had eating disorders.

As I've recovered, however, I have felt a strong desire to help others who have shared in my suffering. I think that if I don't help others, then my pain has been in vain. Telling my story helps make sense of the anorexic experience, both for me and for my fellow sufferers.

Trials

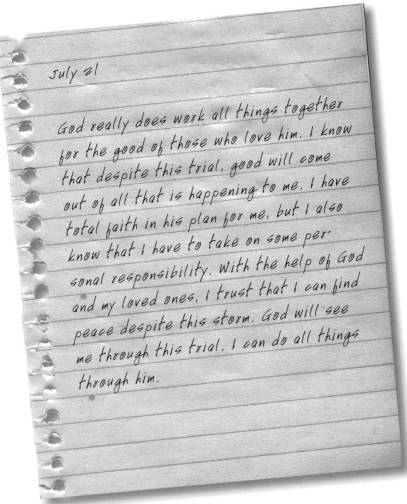

July 21

God really does work all things together for the good of those who love him. I know that despite this trial, good will come out of all that is happening to me. I have total faith in his plan for me, but I also know that I have to take on some personal responsibility. With the help of God and my loved ones, I trust that I can find peace despite this storm. God will see me through this trial. I can do all things through him.

Although I wrote in this entry that I trusted in God's plan for my life, I also assumed that his plan went along with mine. I wanted complete recovery as soon as possible, and I reasoned that God must want this for me as well. I have since learned that God's timetable is not mine. To trust in him does not mean to trust that he will act according to my will. To trust means to let go of my will and accept whatever he has for me, no matter how good or bad the situation may appear to me at the time. Although hard times are just that, there is always something to be learned, and we benefit from our struggles in the end. As Psalm 119:71 says, "It was good for me to be afflicted so that I might learn your decrees."

It was much harder for me to understand why, once I had been through something difficult, God would let me suffer any longer. If I was suffering, then shouldn't he have hurried up and saved me? Clearly,

"In times of desperation, what do we do? We turn to God. And that is what I have to do every day when I am experiencing the constant thought to hate myself for gaining a few pounds or not walking that extra mile at the gym."—Rosie

Trials

I hadn't even begun to see what God was trying to teach me. God needed for me to go through many different stages of recovery to see everything he had for me to learn.

Very often the purpose of suffering is to produce perseverance. As James 1:2–4 says, "Consider it pure joy, my brothers, whenever you face trials of many kinds, because you know that the testing of your faith develops perseverance. Perseverance must finish its work so that you may be mature and complete, not lacking anything." If I was going to make it through recovery, I would have to persevere through the hardest of times.

One of the most important lessons I have been taught through these experiences is about the prayer of surrender. At this point in my recovery I prayed for what I wanted. I wasn't praying for God's will to be done in my life, but rather for him to heal me as quickly as possible. I didn't begin to be freed until I finally gave my problems to him and told him I would suffer for the rest of my life if that was what it would take. It's always important to keep in mind that our sufferings pale in comparison to what Jesus went through for us on the cross. Many times throughout my battle I felt sorry for myself, but God showed me that my suffering could be a good thing if it helped me grow closer to him. It was essential for me to pray for God's will to be done, not my own—this is the prayer of surrender.

Realizing this made me wonder if surrendering my will to God's meant I should no longer pray for the things I desired. This isn't what God wants either. When Jesus was in the Garden of Gethsemane, he prayed that God would take away the suffering he faced. Jesus then proceeded to pray, however, that the Lord's will be done rather than his own. We should imitate Jesus by praying wholeheartedly for what we desire and then let go of our desires and recognize that God's plan is much better than our own. It took me many months to understand this concept. God needed to prolong my suffering until I came to a point spiritually where I was capable of grasping this idea.

Seeking Answers

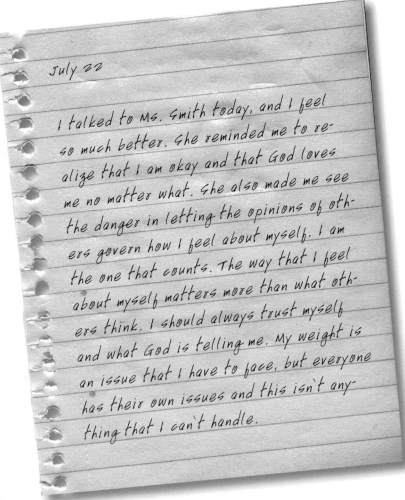

July 22

I talked to Ms. Smith today, and I feel so much better. She reminded me to realize that I am okay and that God loves me no matter what. She also made me see the danger in letting the opinions of others govern how I feel about myself. I am the one that counts. The way that I feel about myself matters more than what others think. I should always trust myself and what God is telling me. My weight is an issue that I have to face, but everyone has their own issues and this isn't anything that I can't handle.

Ms. Smith was my elementary school counselor and the first professional I went to for help about my eating disorder. I decided to call her completely on my own. I knew I needed something to make me feel better. Because I was traveling at the time, I talked to her over the phone. The advice she gave me was good, but unfortunately I twisted it to serve my own purposes. She told me not to worry about the opinions of others. I took that to mean I didn't need to listen when my friends expressed concern about my weight loss. I was still in denial about how serious my problem was, and hearing this made me feel much better. If I could ignore their concern, I could continue to pretend that the problem didn't exist. I certainly didn't want to exercise less and eat more, and if I truly faced my problem I might have to give up my excessive dieting and exercising. I still wasn't ready to really look at my heart and examine why I was being so self-destructive.

"All my life I have had to deal with people telling me I need to lose weight. In middle school I was overweight and the doctor told me I should be active, but I was already playing three sports. I thought I was healthy until junior year when my coach suggested I not eat fried foods."—Casey

"My relationship with my mom has affected my eating the most. There was always a lot of pressure put on appearance. Looks were definitely a definition of character. If you didn't look good and pulled together, that gave people a bad impression of you—that you didn't care enough about yourself."—Amy

Even though I called Ms. Smith, I was also not ready to ask for any real help. Mostly, I just wanted her to tell me I didn't need to worry. It was easy to call her from out of town, because I wouldn't be threatened with having to see her on a regular basis. I thought my issues were more a matter of personal willpower than anything else, and if I was willing to try really hard, then I could will my problem out of my life.

It frightens me now to remember these times. My thoughts were so irrational, and I had absolutely no idea what was really going on. Although I had good intentions, I could not see my situation clearly. Obviously I didn't know what needed to be done to help me, and so much of me didn't even want to be rescued at all. I couldn't figure out how I had gotten so mixed up. When I began to realize that things weren't right, it was as if I suddenly woke up and found myself stuck in a horrible web of confusion.

Failure

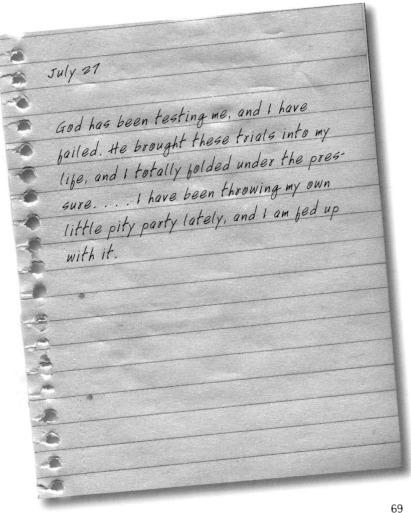

July 21

God has been testing me, and I have failed. He brought these trials into my life, and I totally folded under the pressure. . . . I have been throwing my own little pity party lately, and I am fed up with it.

The more I realized

the depth of my problem, the worse I felt about myself. I couldn't believe I could have ever let myself become a victim of such an irrational disorder. I couldn't understand why I was treating myself so badly, clinging to such destructive habits. This was when the real pain of my eating disorder began. I was stuck in a no-win situation. If I continued in my old habits, I would feel bad about myself because I knew they were unhealthy. If I ate more or exercised less, I would also feel bad about myself because I would fear getting fat. I was caught in a vicious cycle.

I also blamed myself for not being spiritually able to handle what God had given me. As I wrote this entry, I thought I was failing one of God's tests. I felt disconnected from God and spiritually sad. All these feelings came from misconceptions I had about God. I was under the impression that what I did or how I responded to what was happening to me would affect God's love for me. I thought his love was conditional

"I often strive for perfection, and when I fall short of that I'm disappointed in myself. So when I'm not disciplined enough in eating, I feel like a failure. And I don't like to fail."—Jennifer

"I am not that happy with my body. It is a constant struggle to stay in shape. I go back and forth between eating whatever I want and then restricting myself to lose weight. I use exercise as a means to put myself in the shape I desire."—Pamela

"One of my hardest struggles was my continual fall back into sin. I felt so awful constantly messing up. But the freedom I feel now is amazing. I thank God for that, and I try not to fear it happening again."—Lily

and based on my performance. I felt I had not only failed myself but also failed God.

When I battled my eating disorder I had to face, for the first time in my life, my own weaknesses and limitations. It was a humbling experience, and I felt ashamed of my behavior. I was embarrassed that my pain was so evident in my physical appearance. Everyone could see by looking at me that there was something wrong, and that really bothered me. I wanted everyone to think I was successful, well-adjusted, happy, perfect.

I had always been one of those people who seemed to be on top of everything. Now I was faced head-on with my shortcomings. Not only could I see my weakness, but everyone around me could see it as well. Although this experience really broke me down, it was just what I needed. I realized that my weakness is what connects me to others. It is because of my weakness that I am human, just like everyone else, and that I need a Savior. God says in 2 Corinthians 12:9, "My grace is sufficient for you, for my power is made perfect in weakness." It was only in my weakness that I could grasp God's sovereignty.

Up until this point I had always wanted to be the exception to the rule. I did not want to have any downfalls. I wanted to be better than everyone else. I wanted to be perfect—the perfect tennis player, student, daughter, girlfriend. I even wanted to be the perfect Christian. Now I am able to rejoice in my weaknesses, because it is my vulnerability that makes me human, that bonds me with others, and that makes me need Christ so desperately. Struggling with an eating disorder has been one of the most humbling experiences of my life, but God had to break me down in order to show me my need for him.

Sin

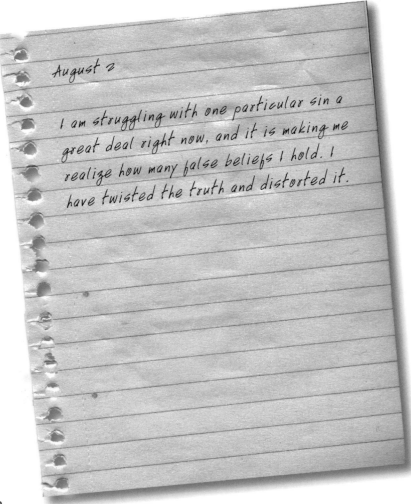

August 2

I am struggling with one particular sin a great deal right now, and it is making me realize how many false beliefs I hold. I have twisted the truth and distorted it.

I am talking about my eating disorder in this passage. I know that *sin* is a word that makes many people uncomfortable, and it holds a variety of connotations, but I can't sidestep this issue. There is no doubt in my mind that my anorexia was a sin—a rebellion against God. My life during my anorexia was not glorifying him and was inconsistent with my beliefs.

The first of the Lord's Ten Commandments tells us that we should have no other gods before him. My weight had become my god, and I was living in sin. There was no way around it. I had taken my anorexia and placed it above God. My weight had become such a central part of my life that it consumed me. I thought about food and working out more than anything else. My whole day revolved around making time for my workouts and being disciplined about what I ate. My mood for the day was based on how well I did these

"I think that seeing how much time and energy I spend thinking about food, exercise, and my weight has definitely revealed some idols in my life. Food and self, as well as exercise, are idols of my heart that I turn to for comfort or when I'm anxious, bored, or stressed. I'm trying to let go of these false gods that give me instant gratification."—Robin

two things. I had replaced my love for God with my love for being skinny.

I began to lose weight with healthy intentions, so when did I cross the line? When did my rebellion against God begin? When did my exercise go from keeping my body in good shape to breaking my body down? How did my originally healthy goals snowball into this obsession?

I think my thoughts became twisted when I let my emotions get involved with my eating and working out. First Corinthians 6:12 says, "'Everything is permissible for me'—but I will not be mastered by anything." I began to draw my emotional self-worth from whether or not I had worked hard enough to lose weight. I let my body become my master. When my weight started to control my life, I lost my focus on God. As my strength and self-worth came more and more from my weight, I let it become an idol in my life.

Because eating disorders are so common today, any girl who starts to take better care of herself and loses weight may be accused of having an eating disorder. "Young women with eating disorders are not all that different from their peers. It's a matter of degree. Almost all adolescent girls feel fat, worry about their weight, diet and feel guilty when they eat" (Pipher 184–85). The question is, where do you draw the line? How do you try to stay fit and take care of your body without taking it too far? When does this lifestyle become sinful?

I still believe that exercise and healthy eating are excellent habits. The body is a temple of God that should be treated as one. I think the important thing to focus on, however, is that your identity and self-worth need to stay separate from your appearance. We cannot judge ourselves based on how well our pants fit or whether or not we restrain ourselves from a tempting dessert. When I let my emotions and my self-worth become involved in my fitness, that was the beginning of the development of my faulty beliefs about myself and about my weight. That is where I crossed the line.

Hard to Change

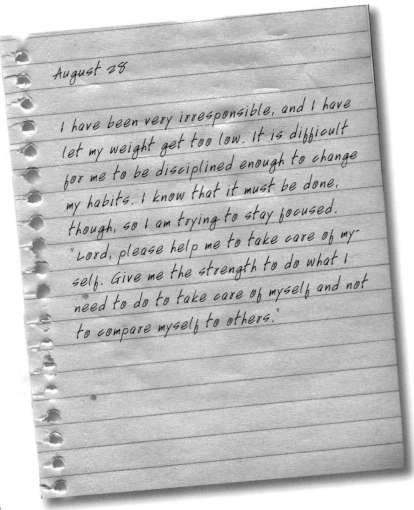

August 28

I have been very irresponsible, and I have
let my weight get too low. It is difficult
for me to be disciplined enough to change
my habits. I know that it must be done,
though, so I am trying to stay focused.
"Lord, please help me to take care of myself. Give me the strength to do what I
need to do to take care of myself and not
to compare myself to others."

For someone with an eating disorder, gaining weight is a major challenge. I was torn between wanting to stay skinny and wanting to be healthy again. It was especially difficult for me to gain weight because I continued to exercise intensely. With my workouts and my tennis practices, I had to make sure I consumed enough calories every day, and to gain weight I had to almost double the amount of food I ate.

This is where a nutritionist was helpful. At the end of the summer, I decided on my own to see a nutritionist, thinking I needed to make some minor adjustments to my diet to stop losing weight. She showed me how much I had been undereating and gave me a plan to gradually build my weight. The first time I went to see the nutritionist I remember thinking she was nuts—that she just wanted to make me fat. I thought she was overweight (like just about everyone else, according to my ridiculous standards), and I

"I focus too much on exercise and not enough on my relationship with God. You need to be satisfied with your body and realize that God made you for a reason. I have a problem with trying to burn off what I have eaten."—Ellen

"I feel sad about how I've gained weight, and then I want to eat to make myself feel better. Overeating has become a habit, and now I feel like it's too hard to change and stop eating as much as I do. I feel like giving up chocolate and sweets is impossible because it is the biggest pleasure in my life."—Tina

Hard to Change

wasn't about to let her make me look like that too. She gave me a sample diet, what a normal day of eating should consist of, and I laughed at it. I thought I could never possibly eat as much as she expected me to. Although I only met with her a couple of times, the guidance she gave me eventually helped me straighten out my diet. Looking back, her suggestions were completely reasonable, and I still refer to the information she gave me.

To change my eating habits, I had to make gradual adjustments. For example, when I was dieting I would drink nothing but water. The nutritionist suggested I add juices and Gatorade to my diet to help me get extra calories without feeling full. I struggled the most with needing control over exactly what and how much I ate. I insisted on measuring out exactly how many pretzels I would let myself eat. Over time I began to allow myself as much as I wanted, but I didn't trust myself to accurately determine when I had enough. At first, these changes made me afraid I would gain too much weight, but then I got used to them. A little later I was ready to take on some other changes like adding more meat back into my diet. Bit by bit I was able to raise my intake enough that I gained weight while still eating relatively healthy foods.

To gain weight I had to eat an extra meal every day. Before I went to bed I would have another meal to make up for the calories I might have missed during the day. I usually ate until I was full, but this would often make me feel uncomfortable. I feared that I was bound to be getting fat with all I was eating. It was hard to make myself keep eating so much more food than I had become accustomed to. I didn't want to give up the control I had been thriving on, but I knew that was what I needed to do to reclaim my life.

I had convinced myself that foods like eggs and cheese and pasta would make me fat. It took discipline to prove to myself that those foods were good for me. My nutritionist even told me I needed to start eating fewer fruits and vegetables. How could that be true? What food could be better than fruits and vegetables? My nutritionist explained that I was filling my stomach with food that didn't have the calories I needed.

One of the most difficult eating habits for me to change was breaking out of the "fat-free" mentality. There are fat-free alternatives for just about every food imaginable, and I believed that choosing the fat-free food was always the healthiest alternative. Although it is good to have a diet that isn't high in fat, I had almost none in mine. My nutritionist told me I needed to increase my fat intake from about ten grams of fat a day to fifty grams. It was hard for me to stop buying the fat-free alternatives. I was convinced that fat in food would translate into fat on my body. Learning to incorporate more fat into my diet is the perfect example of how I had to redefine what it means to be healthy.

Exhausted

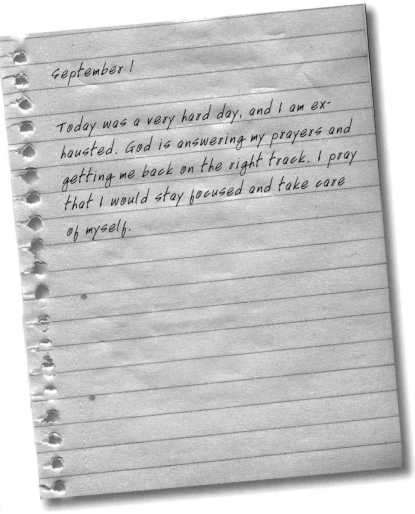

September 1

Today was a very hard day, and I am ex-
hausted. God is answering my prayers and
getting me back on the right track. I pray
that I would stay focused and take care
of myself.

Working on my recovery was one of the most exhausting things I've ever been through. Habits, whether good or bad, are difficult to break. I had to face my problem every time I put food into my mouth. It was a relentless process, and many times I wanted to quit. I wanted to just remain in the comfort of my self-destruction and continue to feed off of the satisfaction of being obsessively disciplined. I never realized how long it would take or how hard it would be to get better.

Some days were better than others. There were many times when I just wanted to escape from it all. People who are addicted to alcohol can abstain from drinking completely and more or less get away from alcohol. But victims of eating disorders must eat at least three times a day and are forced to deal with their problem at every meal. Surprisingly, it took more willpower to make myself eat more

"I battle every day with what I can and can't eat!"—Glenda

and gain weight than it did for me to eat less and lose weight in the first place.

When I was battling back from anorexia, I often felt tired and weak, as I wrote in this entry. It wasn't so much a physical tiredness as it was an emotional one. It was so difficult to fight my habits day in and day out that sometimes I felt like I just didn't have the strength to fight anymore. When I felt so weak, I turned to God for my strength. Knowing that he was behind me and supporting me helped me to face my anorexia again day after day. I was encouraged daily with verses such as Hebrews 10:39, which says, "But we are not of those who shrink back and are destroyed, but of those who believe and are saved." As time went by it got easier, and I didn't feel so tired. I learned that perseverance is essential to the recovery process.

Support

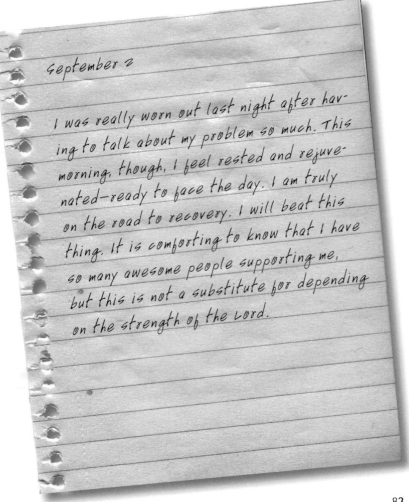

September 2

I was really worn out last night after having to talk about my problem so much. This morning, though, I feel rested and rejuvenated—ready to face the day. I am truly on the road to recovery. I will beat this thing. It is comforting to know that I have so many awesome people supporting me, but this is not a substitute for depending on the strength of the Lord.

When I arrived back at school after not seeing my friends for three months, many people expressed concern for me. By now my bones were jutting out of my body. It was impossible not to notice my weight loss. The last five pounds I lost over the summer made quite a difference in my appearance. It was not as noticeable to me, but people who had not seen me for three months were worried. Everyone wanted to talk to me about what was going on. I have always been open about my eating disorder, so I didn't mind trying to explain to them. But how do you explain to someone why you are intentionally starving yourself?

Because I did not yet understand what I was going through, these conversations usually didn't help much. I'm sure my friends could see that I was still denying my problem. I would tell them that I wanted to gain weight, but I didn't really mean it yet. Mostly I just didn't want there to be anything wrong with me.

During this time I ended up having to talk about my eating to at

"Listen to the words that you tell other people—that beauty is so much more than being thin. And listen to the words that they tell you—that you are so much more than this struggle."—Kara

"I have wonderful friends who have encouraged me and loved me unconditionally even when my parents haven't. What I have to work on now is forgiving and not blaming."—Grace

How to Help Someone Who Is Struggling

1. Recognize the signs and symptoms of eating disorders and understand you are not alone in having to address these issues.
2. Focus on feelings and relationships not on weight and food.
3. Convey concern for her health while still respecting the person's privacy. Eating disorders are often a cry for help, and the individual will appreciate knowing that someone is concerned.
4. Avoid commenting on appearance; the person is already overly focused on this.
5. Demanding change or criticizing the person for her eating habits will not work. If you try to tell her what to do, she may do the opposite.
6. Realize that the individual needs to work at her own pace in getting better. By providing information and being supportive, you are helping her to see and consider alternatives to the present situation. Don't try to rush the individual to eat more or gain weight. This is a process that will occur over time.
7. Examine your own attitudes about food, weight, body image, and body size to ensure you do not make negative comments about weight or increase the person's desire to be thin.
8. Find alternatives to current ways of communication. For example, stay calm instead of raising your voice if the conversation becomes tense.
9. Be careful not to blame the person for her struggle. Try to understand eating problems as a way to deal with painful emotions or experiences.
10. Gather together a group of people to help, including a nutritionist, counselor, teachers, parents, and friends.
11. Do not take on the role of a therapist. Just be a friend and encourage her to seek counseling.

Adapted from the National Eating Disorder Information Centre (of Canada)

least one person every day. As I wrote in my journal, this was exhausting. Constantly being confronted just made me want to escape from the whole thing. I know it was an important part of my recovery process to share with others and try to express my feelings, but it was absolutely consuming my life.

Support

It seemed like all I ever thought about or talked about was my eating disorder. I was continually hurt by what my life had become.

It also bothered me that the first thing anyone thought of when they looked at me was that I was anorexic. My old self had been completely lost. Who was I now? I felt like nothing more than the girl with the eating disorder.

Although all of this was emotionally draining, I had hope again for the first time. I would wake up each day with a determination to fight and win my battle. When I felt like I was too tired to fight, God would build me up and help me press on. For example, these words seemed to speak directly to me: "Be strong and courageous, and do the work. Do not be afraid or discouraged, for the LORD God, my God, is with you. He will not fail you or forsake you until all the work for the service of the temple of the LORD is finished" (1 Chron. 28:20). God was my strength through this hard time.

God helped me through those around me. I had so many wonderful people in my life to encourage me. I am so thankful for that. I don't know how they endured me at times, but whenever I needed to talk, my friends and family were always there for me. My brother, my mom, and my dad listened to me complain about what I was going through. My boyfriend, Peter, whom I had been dating for about six months, stood by me and encouraged me daily. My closest friends at school were patient and supportive. I can imagine how hard it was for them. They couldn't really understand what I was going through, but they stood by me anyway. With so many wonderful people around me, I knew recovery was worth fighting for. I wanted to get better so I could enjoy life with my loved ones again. I definitely could never have recovered without the love and support of the wonderful people around me.

There were times when support from friends and family was of the utmost importance to me. There were also times when there was nothing anyone could do for me. Eventually, the victim of an eating disorder has to face her problems head-on. The motivation to do this comes from within, from the support of others, and from God. If you have a friend who suffers from an eating disorder, it is certainly important to be there for her, but she has to be there for herself as well.

Breaking Through

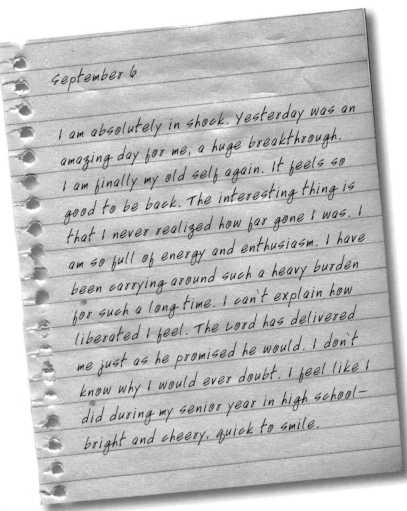

September 6

I am absolutely in shock. Yesterday was an amazing day for me, a huge breakthrough. I am finally my old self again. It feels so good to be back. The interesting thing is that I never realized how far gone I was. I am so full of energy and enthusiasm. I have been carrying around such a heavy burden for such a long time. I can't explain how liberated I feel. The Lord has delivered me just as he promised he would. I don't know why I would ever doubt. I feel like I did during my senior year in high school—bright and cheery, quick to smile.

This was the first time in a long time that I really felt good again. It was so wonderful to feel happy and not overwhelmed by my obsession. After having food and my weight be the only thing I could think about for such a long time, it was liberating to feel so happy and not distracted by my problem. Unfortunately, however, there were both positive and negative aspects to beginning to feel good again.

Feeling happy was wonderful because it gave me incentive to fight my anorexia. It was hard work, but once I realized that I could really get my life back, I dedicated myself to nothing short of a full recovery. I know a lot of girls who have struggled with their weight their whole lives. I didn't want to let that happen to me. I really wanted to beat this thing. Feeling happy again gave me hope that recovery was possible. Galatians 6:9 says, "Let us not become weary in doing good, for at the proper time we will reap a harvest if we do not give up." Although this

"What really helped me to start feeling better was realizing that each body was created differently, that God delights in his creation, and that he does not want us to be carbon copies of one another. I have to remind myself that I am not in competition with anyone. You must be very strong and convinced of this in your own mind and not be swayed by the words, actions, behavior, or thoughts of others."—Nicki

was only the beginning of my harvest, it gave me the hope and encouragement I would need to press on.

Feeling better also helped me by showing me how severe my problem really was. Before this experience I hadn't realized how different I had really become. Because I was always so tired from working out, so weak from being hungry, and so stressed out about getting fat, I had become a different person—one who wasn't happy or fun to be around. Because it was such a gradual change, I hadn't been aware of it. All the life was just seeping out of me. I had forgotten how joyful and energetic I used to be. I had forgotten what it was like to be me. Now that I could see the difference between who I once was and who I had become, it frightened me. This vision of what my life had been and what it should be now made me commit myself again to recovering. I didn't want to spend the rest of my life feeling like this.

In a way, this discovery of how much my eating disorder had affected me was the lowest point in my entire struggle. Up until this time I hadn't faced what I was up against. Now I knew how low I was and how far I had to climb to get out of the mess I was in. I was afraid I wouldn't have the strength to get myself out. I was mad at myself for letting this happen to me. I was embarrassed by who I had become, and I didn't know if I would ever be the same again. I was scared, really scared.

This good day that I wrote about in my journal was the beginning of a difficult roller-coaster ride. *Overcoming an eating disorder is a long and difficult process with many ups and downs.* At this time I thought I was much better because I'd had such a good day, but I didn't realize how many low days would follow. I had no idea at the time how hard my recovery would be.

What Is Beneath the Surface?

Once I had begun to be able to identify the problem that I was facing, it was time to take the next step in recovery. This was when the real work began. As I became more aware of how serious my problem was and how much it was controlling my life, I realized that I would need professional help. My counselor was able to help me sort through the deeper issues that were beneath the surface of my eating disorder. I came to understand that my unhealthy relationship with food and exercise was an external symptom of deeper things that I was struggling with. In the following section, I ask myself the question, What is beneath the surface?

Getting Help

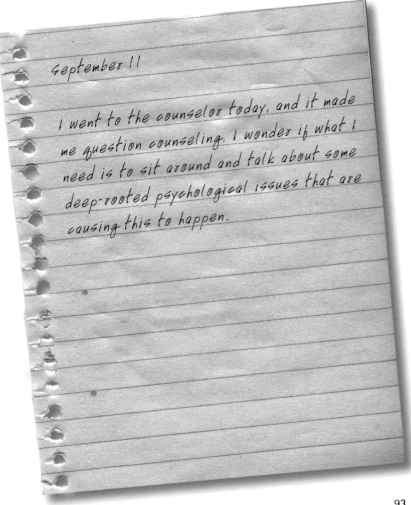

September 11

I went to the counselor today, and it made me question counseling. I wonder if what I need is to sit around and talk about some deep-rooted psychological issues that are causing this to happen.

When I returned to school that fall, my college tennis coach was extremely worried about me. We had always been close and been able to talk about almost anything, so when he confronted me about my weight loss I was receptive to his concerns. He explained to me that the NCAA has guidelines for how to handle suspected weight problems. He asked me to go to student health services to get a physical, to see a nutritionist, and to have a consultation with a counselor. Because I was ready to understand my continued weight loss and heightened anxiety about my weight, I willingly made the appointments.

The checkup confirmed that I was underweight and that I was exercising too much. The doctors were concerned that I was at risk of a heart attack because my heartbeat was slightly irregular and extremely slow. My blood pressure was also low. Since I had already been to a nutritionist once, I returned to the same woman for several more appoint-

"During my senior year in college I went to see a Christian counselor. She helped me to see the spiritual, family, and relationship issues that ran deep and affected the way that I viewed myself. I also began to come out of hiding with my problems and started to open up to my close friends about my struggles, which then allowed others to encourage me in the ways that I needed to be encouraged."—Opal

ments so that she could help me restructure my diet. Visiting the counselor was intimidating, but I tried to be honest and hear what she had to say about my condition. She confirmed that I was anorexic and scheduled an appointment for me to begin weekly counseling sessions. My experience with the counselor taught me a lot about myself.

As a psychology and religious studies major, I thought a lot about how the two fields both contradict and complement one another. I was skeptical that going to a counselor would really help me and wondered if I should continue going. Looking back now, I am glad I stuck with it. Without professional help I would never be where I am today.

My problem with the counseling in the beginning was that it took so long for my counselor and me to get to know each other. Progress seemed slow at first, especially since I was so eager to be cured. In the beginning, each session was spent with me explaining the kinds of things I thought about. The counselor didn't make many comments, and I wasn't sure what I was supposed to be saying. Eventually, though, the counselor started to give me more suggestions about what might be going on in my life.

Throughout the early struggles in counseling, my spiritual life always influenced how I viewed my problem. I could sense that much of my problem came out of spiritual misconceptions that could be corrected. I wish my counselor had been a Christian so that we could have talked more openly about my spiritual life. The counselor always listened to and accepted what I said about how God related to my problem, but we did not connect on this level. I think that combining religion and psychology is beneficial and that biblical counseling would have been good for me.

Needing Balance

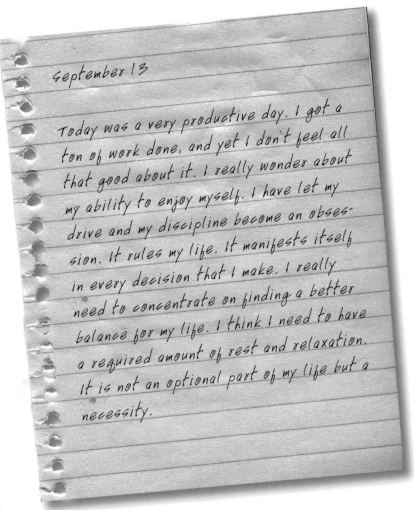

September 13

Today was a very productive day. I got a ton of work done, and yet I don't feel all that good about it. I really wonder about my ability to enjoy myself. I have let my drive and my discipline become an obsession. It rules my life. It manifests itself in every decision that I make. I really need to concentrate on finding a better balance for my life. I think I need to have a required amount of rest and relaxation. It is not an optional part of my life but a necessity.

Meeting and talking

with my counselor showed me that I have an obsessive-compulsive personality. I have always been a perfectionist and a hard worker. Up until this time I had always viewed my discipline and drive as positive attributes. My greatest strength was also now my greatest weakness. I didn't realize how dangerous this trait can be until my disciplined personality led me to an eating disorder.

Certain types of people are more likely to get eating disorders, and perfectionists are definitely among that group. "Type A" personalities, or people who tend to be disciplined, driven, and organized, are often the ones afflicted with eating problems. I had always been obsessive about being the best I could be. In my mind, success in every aspect of my life was a worthy goal. But my eating disorder showed me that my life was not balanced.

Over the past year I had applied my intense discipline to my body—what I ate and how much I exercised. It was not only in

"I feel like my body is average, but I strive to have a model-like body that is perfect in my eyes. I don't really restrict myself from what I want to eat, but I constantly think about calories and fat. I would like to feel satisfied with my body—like it was beautiful and I didn't always have 'problem areas.'"—Wendy

"Exercise often takes over all of my time and energy. I'm never satisfied with my physical appearance, and I have some type of 'unreachable ideal' shape in my head. I would like to be at peace with my appearance and not always concerned with such unimportant things."—Allison

"My thoughts were consumed by my exercise. I would at times catch myself in conversation with someone and I hadn't heard anything they had said because I was thinking about how long or when I would next be exercising."—Stephanie

my eating habits, however, that my discipline had taken over my life. The same thing that caused me to eat the way I did also caused me to study too much, work out too much, and rarely let myself relax. I was constantly looking for ways to improve myself. I was only happy when I was spending my time productively. When I realized how intense every aspect of my life had become, I knew my eating habits were not the only thing that needed to change. My obsessive-compulsive tendencies, which were at the root of my eating disorder, needed to be addressed.

My anorexia was an outward expression of a large problem in my life. It was a relief to recognize what was at the root of my disorder. At least now I had a better understanding of what I was up against. Although it seemed overwhelming to think that there were so many things about the way I was living that needed to be fixed, it was comforting to be able to identify the problem. With the help of my counselor, I now felt more equipped to fight my perfectionism and its control over my life.

A Long Way to Go

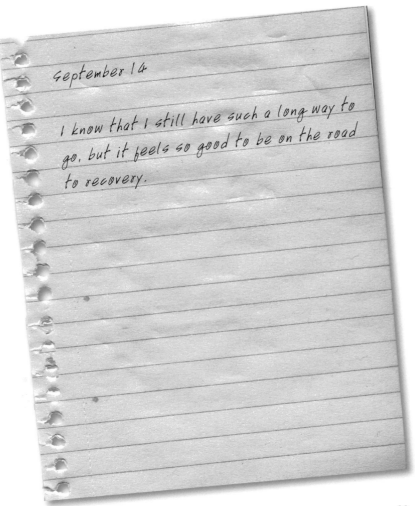

September 14

I know that I still have such a long way to
go, but it feels so good to be on the road
to recovery.

The irony of this statement was that I had no idea how far I really had to go. I have been surprised how long it has taken me to recover. *Fighting an eating disorder is definitely a process of baby steps.* It took me about nine months to form my bad habits, but it has taken over three years to break them. It was difficult for me to define precisely what normal habits were, but I knew that I had to let go of the ones I knew were self-destructive.

Throughout my recovery it seemed that for every three steps I took forward, I took one step back. A good day or week was inevitably followed by a bad one. As more time passed, though, the good times seemed to become more frequent than the bad. As I wrote in this entry, I was just glad to be getting back on the right track. I had to emphasize the signs of improvement so that I would not get discouraged in my struggle. I used my improvements as encouragement when I was feeling down and ready to quit.

"Once you have experienced those feelings, it is hard to turn back into your 'old' self. So much of your life has now been trained to think in terms of pounds, miles run, and calories consumed. I have to keep my body image in check and often fail miserably."—Virginia

No matter what I faced, I could never give up hope. When I was in the midst of my struggle, I didn't know how long it would take for me to get better or if I would ever truly recover at all. I remember wishing I could just know that in six weeks or six months or six years, I would be over my eating disorder. I was told that most people who have an eating disorder struggle with it their whole life. That was my biggest fear. I was determined not to be obsessed with food and weight forever.

I don't believe that once you have an eating disorder you are doomed forever. I believe God allowed me to develop an eating disorder for a reason. I also know that since God is all-powerful, he has the power to free me from this burden whenever he thinks is best. It could be that God wants me to be anorexic for the rest of my life so I can learn from it and help others. It could be that God wants me to deal with this now, and then he will have me move on to other challenges. There is no way I can know God's perfect plan for my life. I am certain, though, that God's plan is far better for me than anything I could ever plan for myself. By trusting in his plan for my life, I am able to strive for recovery without getting frustrated and losing hope. I know that he is watching over me.

Comparison

September 17

Proverbs 20:23 says, "Dishonest scales do not please him." This passage has spoken to me in an interesting way this morning. I have been hurting God by how much I compare myself to other people. My worth is not relative to others. When comparing myself to others, it is as if I am trying to see the bad in them so that I can build myself up. This is especially true with my weight. I should be only looking for the good in others, looking to see God in them. It is so cool that God has spoken to me in this way through this Scripture. It is obviously something that is important to him and should be to me. Even today, just after what God taught me this morning, I already found myself comparing myself to others. It is a horrible habit that I have developed. I feel like I have to exercise more and eat less than everyone around me. I really want to let go of this. I don't have to be the best; I just have to be me. When I am around my peers I always find myself comparing myself to them—to sort of check how I am doing. I need to readjust my thinking, realizing that I am loved as a child of God, just as I am, and how I compare to others does not matter in any sense.

Throughout my recovery, God taught me lessons like this one about making comparisons. Even though my eating disorder has been the hardest thing I've ever gone through, it has also been one of the biggest blessings in my life because of how God used it to teach me. We all have areas in our lives that we need to work on, and God is constantly molding us into his servants. It was at my weakest point that I was most open to change.

My competitive nature has shown itself at various times throughout my life. In the past I had always used sports as my competitive outlet. As I was growing up, I never compared what I ate or my figure to others. I had always been oblivious to what others ate. When I went to college, however, I began to eat every meal with my friends. That was when I noticed, for the first time, how little they ate in comparison to me.

As this journal entry shows, I constantly compared myself to other girls. The first thing I noticed about a girl was how skinny she was. When I ate with my friends, I always had to order the healthiest thing on the menu. I would feel uncomfortable if someone ordered something healthier or ate less than I did. I felt I had to exercise more than anyone else on my tennis team. I don't know how I ever developed this habit, but when I realized what I was doing, I was absolutely sickened by my behavior.

It is important to learn that when it comes to what our bodies need to live on, we are all very different. My competitive eating habits led to my

"I find I compare myself with my friends—in some ways that makes me feel better about myself and in some ways that makes me feel worse."—Stacy

"Comparison is the thief of *all* joy, and that is the root of who I am. I compare myself to everyone around me, and I consistently never measure up because I am overweight."—Melissa

"I guess it was the competitive nature in me. I wasn't comparing myself to others as much as I was comparing myself to me—the new me and the old me, the thin me and the bigger me. I guess I thought being skinny meant being a better person."—Bonnie

What Is Beneath the Surface?

rapid weight loss. It was hard for me to see that I wasn't getting enough calories because I was eating just like my friends who were not Division I college athletes.

Girls tend to put a lot of pressure on each other to have similar eating habits. Once I fell into the trap of being aware of what everyone around me was eating, I was in a bad situation. *Eating is not a competitive sport.* It is meant to be a social event, but when I was constantly comparing myself to others, I couldn't enjoy it. The bottom line is that it doesn't matter what the people around me do and do not eat. I have to listen to my body and give it what it wants.

When I noticed my need to be the skinniest and eat the healthiest, I could see how my eating disorder was a result of my insecurities. Because I was no longer comfortable with who I was, feeling skinny was the only way I could feel good about myself. Lisa Bevere experienced similar feelings during her own struggles with an eating disorder: "I saw how I had drawn strength from my weight and not from God. I measured myself by the scales, determining that I was worthy of love if I was thin but not if I was fat" (124). I had also programmed myself to think that I was somehow a better person now because I was skinnier than I used to be.

In high school, I considered myself to be one of the more self-confident girls in my class. My tennis, my family, my friends, my faith, and my schoolwork had always made me feel secure about myself. When I left for college and went to a new place where no one knew who I was, I felt threatened. It was as if all of a sudden I didn't know who I was anymore. I was lost without the daily support and encouragement of my family. I wasn't sure where I was going to fit in at college, and as a result my self-confidence gradually disappeared. I

Comparison

started to use dieting and weight loss as a way to deal with my insecurities. Losing weight was a superficial way for me to feel good about myself.

As you can see, *eating disorders are about much more than just food.* Through my experience, God taught me that it is not good to be constantly comparing myself to others in any way. My identity and my self-confidence should not come from being skinnier than everyone else, from being a really good tennis player, or even from having supportive parents. My self-confidence has to come from my identity in Christ and the security of God's unconditional love for me. "Your beauty should not come from outward adornment, such as braided hair and the wearing of gold jewelry and fine clothes. Instead, it should be that of your inner self, the unfading beauty of a gentle and quiet spirit, which is of great worth in God's sight" (1 Peter 3:3–4). I learned that I needed to rest my identity on my inner self alone.

I have never met a person who is exactly like me. God made each and every one of us different. We are all special and unique. My goal is to celebrate differences rather than constantly compare myself to others. To enjoy my uniqueness, I must first be comfortable with myself. If I am secure in my identity in Christ, then I will be able to appreciate the strengths and weaknesses of those around me. This is one of the most valuable lessons that God has taught me through my eating disorder.

Moderation

September 20

I am having a lot of trouble finding moderation in my life. "If you find honey, eat just enough—too much of it, and you will vomit" (Prov. 25:16). Notice in this verse that God does not tell us not to have any honey—he wants for us to enjoy the pleasures of the world. But he also warns of having too much. It is all about moderation. This verse can be applied to so many different areas of my life—food, spending time with my boyfriend, spending time with friends. The problem is that often I do not make good judgments about what is enough. I get a set idea in my mind of what is appropriate (which often isn't much), and then I feel guilty if I have more than that. I would like to find moderation in my life.

The first thing that should be noticed about this entry (and the previous entry) is how God was guiding me through my recovery with his Word. Even though the Bible was written over two thousand years ago when anorexia was not yet a named disorder, I could still find verses that seemed to speak directly to me about my problem. I had been praying for God's help with my eating disorder for quite some time, and one way that he answered my prayers was by leading me to specific advice in the Bible. I was beginning to see the truth in David's words: "A righteous man may have many troubles, but the LORD delivers him from them all" (Ps. 34:19). God supported me through this difficult time with Scripture.

My counselor and I talked a lot about finding moderation in my life. My life had been out of balance for a long time, but it took the outward symptom of my eating disorder for me to see how off-balance it was. Even in

"Sometimes exercise consumes me and becomes an obsession. I am scared to stop exercising because of how that would affect my weight. I would like to feel in control and like my body is a temple worthy of the Holy Spirit."—Carol

What Is Beneath the Surface?

high school I studied excessively and spent too much time on the tennis court. I did not spend enough time hanging out with friends or just relaxing. I had the type of personality that made me want to achieve, and to me that meant investing almost all my time in working toward my goals.

When I got to college my quest to achieve only got worse. At the University of Virginia, I suddenly found myself surrounded by others who had all achieved as much as I had in high school. If I wanted to stand out in college, I was going to have to work even harder than before. I had to face the reality that I wasn't going to have the highest GPA at the University of Virginia or play number one on the tennis team. When I discovered this, I subconsciously decided that I needed to find another way to set myself apart.

Because many people gain weight in college, I realized that I could be different by being in better shape than my peers. Instead of gaining weight like everyone else, I could lose weight. I threw myself into achieving in the realm of fitness so that I could feel special. I wanted to be the fittest, the leanest, the thinnest. I had to be the best at *something*.

Because I was unable to find moderation, extremes became dangerous in my life. Moderation can be a challenge for someone who is striving to be the best. There is a point at which more isn't necessarily better, and, unfortunately, I lost sight of that. Thankfully, through the wisdom of the Bible and with the help of my counselor, I began to see the importance of moderation. I still struggle with finding moderation in many activities, but this is another area of my life where God used my eating disorder to show me where I needed to change.

Isolation

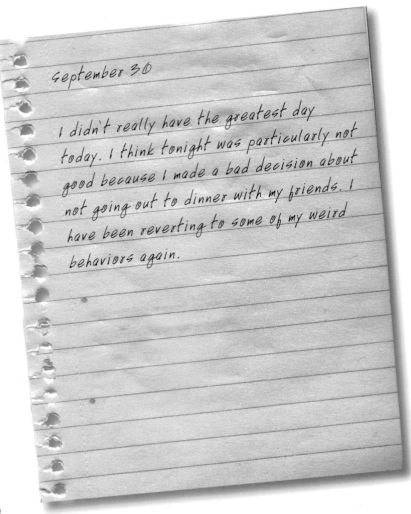

September 30

I didn't really have the greatest day today. I think tonight was particularly not good because I made a bad decision about not going out to dinner with my friends. I have been reverting to some of my weird behaviors again.

One of the most troubling side effects of my eating disorder was how it affected my social life. When I began to see how my problem was coming between my friends and me, it upset me. For example, I remember halfheartedly accepting invitations from my boyfriend to go out to lunch. He was patient with my reluctance and didn't take it too personally, although at times he would get frustrated with my attitude. I was falling in love with him and wanted to want to go out to eat with him, but my awful relationship with food held me back.

Because I had made up rules about what I could and could not eat, there were many times when I felt like I couldn't enjoy food with my boyfriend or my friends. I had to live by a different set of standards. Maybe my friends could eat pizza, but I certainly couldn't. I looked down on people who ate things like french fries and real ice cream. I thought they had no self-control. Finally I realized that I was the

"I don't like eating in front of boys. I wish I could fully accept the way I look and not worry too much about what I eat. I wish I could be okay with eating in front of people, not just boys."—Melanie

"I have a few times feared going out to eat because I did not want to be stopped from eating my normal meal. I have to have control and time to do and eat when and what I want, and that is a problem."—Julia

"I began to realize how my exercise habits were negatively affecting my relationships with people I cared about, and I wanted to change. I definitely am not at a point where I am totally flexible in my routine, but it does progressively get better with effort."—Jamie

"When I feel the worst about my body I am totally depressed. All I think about is my shortcomings and imperfections. It makes it hard to hang out with friends because I am so utterly consumed with feeling fat."—Christina

one with the problem, not them. Even though I had already seen a nutritionist and had begun to work on improving my diet, I still set many rules to control my intake.

My restrictions on what I would allow myself to eat soon applied to how much money I would spend on food. After developing my eating disorder, I wouldn't go out to eat with friends, because I didn't want to waste money. I thought food wasn't worth spending money on, and I thought *I* wasn't worth spending money on. Feeling uncomfortable about spending money on food for myself was another area that showed my low self-esteem.

I saw food and eating as a waste of my time. I thought I was too busy to spend a whole hour out to dinner with my friends. Marya Hornbacher describes how sometimes it can make you feel important if you are so busy that you don't have time to eat (118). This is a common problem with perfection-istic, overproductive anorexics. I thought I was above food. I wanted to be superhuman.

Another interesting aspect of my anorexia was that I had a harder and harder time making decisions. I used to be an extraordinarily decisive person—I always knew what I wanted—but then I started to make irrational decisions about food and exercise. It became a big issue for me to decide what I would eat, because I would ignore what my body was telling me it wanted. I didn't know how to look at a menu and decide what would really taste good to me. I would take ages trying to decide which items on the menu contained the fewest fat grams or calories. I often regretted the decisions I made about food, as this journal entry shows. My eating disorder clouded my judgment.

Guilt

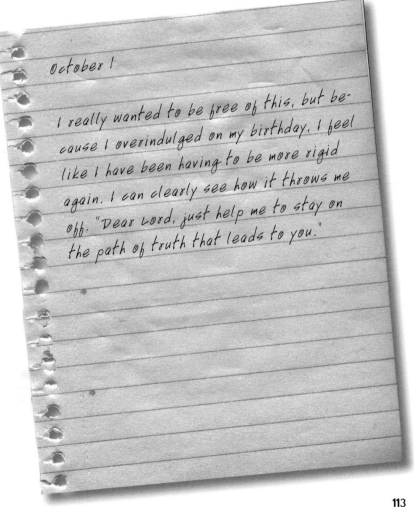

October 1

I really wanted to be free of this, but because I overindulged on my birthday, I feel like I have been having to be more rigid again. I can clearly see how it throws me off. "Dear Lord, just help me to stay on the path of truth that leads to you."

During my recovery

I was often plagued with a sense of guilt and low self-esteem. The one emotion I most closely associate with food is guilt. Eating made me feel guilty. Because I felt so guilty after eating fattening food, I couldn't enjoy many foods at all. Foods that I had previously enjoyed didn't taste good to me because of the guilt I felt after eating them. I couldn't enjoy nice dinners with my family or go out on dates with my boyfriend because I would feel so guilty for what I had eaten. I was afraid of food, and I hated the way eating made me feel about myself. These were the feelings I would have to conquer if I was going to regain a normal relationship with food and overcome my anorexia.

Once I knew I had to gain weight, I had to learn to rationalize the guilt away. I had to reassure myself that I needed to eat more substantial foods if I was ever going to gain any weight. Most of the time I could make the guilt go away, but sometimes

"Sometime I get disgusted with myself when I eat so much. Sometimes I feel gluttonous. It's horrible, but I can't help it. I feel guilty for eating so much, yet at the same time, I'm not disciplined enough to stop eating."—Caroline

"I am terribly scared of gaining weight and becoming fat when I am older. After I exercise I feel skinnier, and if I haven't exercised in a while I feel fat. I hate trying on five different outfits and feeling so ugly and gross looking."—Valerie

it threw me off, as I described in this journal entry. Over time, with a great deal of discipline, I was able to learn to eat without feeling guilty.

This journal entry addresses another problem I faced as I began to recover. For my birthday I received lots of treats such as candy, cake, and brownies. For a long time I hadn't allowed myself to eat such indulgent foods. Now, as I realized I needed to gain weight, I knew I could start eating these foods that I had labeled "off-limits."

Because I had deprived myself of the sweets I loved for so long, when I allowed myself to eat them, I didn't know when to stop. When I was given a plate of brownies for my birthday, I couldn't eat just one. I ate too many, and then I felt sick to my stomach and guilty for having shown so little self-control. Afterward I felt like I had to cleanse myself by making my next few meals lighter. When I overate like this, I would also make myself exercise more to take away the guilt. Thankfully, I never experimented with making myself vomit, but I would spend extra time at the gym or eat lighter after I felt I had indulged. *It is not uncommon, however, for recovering anorexics to become bulimic as they begin to eat more.*

I have read a lot about bingeing and purging, and I don't think I had a serious problem with it. I wasn't actually bingeing, but I felt like I was because I was used to eating so little food. As a result, when I ate more normal amounts, or even too much, I felt badly about it. I knew in my mind that in order to gain weight I was going to have to overeat, but I was surprised how it affected me emotionally. I wanted to gain weight, but I didn't like how eating so much made me feel both physically and emotionally. My stomach had shrunk so much that it was uncomfortable for me to eat as much as I needed to.

After overeating for many days in a row in an attempt to gain weight, I felt like I needed a break. I think it was good for me to take these little breaks so that I could regroup and be ready for my next big step forward. Over the course of the past years I've seen how my recovery came in stages like this. It was okay for me to take a day or two off from trying to gain weight as long as I was diligent and started back again soon. This allowed for my gradual weight gain.

Even though I felt like I was stuffing myself every day, it still took me an entire year to gain ten pounds. I think I gained the weight in a healthy way, because I put it on gradually and became more and more comfortable with a bigger me. I kept exercising and steadily increased the amount of food I was comfortable eating. I kept eating mostly healthy foods, but I incorporated more hearty meals of proteins, carbohydrates, and moderate fats. I was surprised how difficult it was to gain weight and how purposeful I had to be in my efforts.

After talking to other girls about their experiences, however, I have realized that everyone's recovery is different. When someone with anorexia is trying to overcome it and gain weight, she has to find what works for her. Every eating disorder, as well as every recovery, takes its own unique form. Unfortunately, I can't prescribe a set formula for how to gain weight after anorexia; I can only describe my personal experiences.

Control

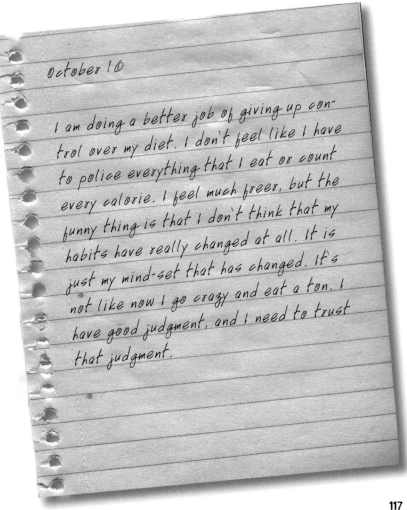

October 10

I am doing a better job of giving up control over my diet. I don't feel like I have to police everything that I eat or count every calorie. I feel much freer, but the funny thing is that I don't think that my habits have really changed at all. It is just my mind-set that has changed. It's not like now I go crazy and eat a ton. I have good judgment, and I need to trust that judgment.

I took comfort in the control I was able to exert over my diet, and not having that control frightened me. I needed to feel like I had control over what I ate because I had so little control over everything else that was going on in my life. When I left for school, I couldn't control the fact that I couldn't see my family very often. I also couldn't control my grades like I could in high school. Even my best effort wouldn't ensure an A the way it always had before. I also couldn't control where I was going to play in the tennis lineup. I couldn't control whether or not I felt accepted and liked by my new group of friends. In response to all these changes, I clung to the control I *could* have. I sought comfort in control over my diet.

As I noted in this entry, letting go of control of my diet didn't change my habits much. I had always been afraid that once I gave up my control, I would eat way too much. Because I had controlled my diet

"I think that the desire to achieve perfection through controlling my life is the underlying issue that causes my struggles."—Courtney

"Weight was a constant struggle between me and my mom. It pretty much boiled down to her wanting control and me not letting her have it. The unfortunate part of it is that I felt being a certain size was the condition by which I would either be approved or not by my parents, a boy, or anyone else for that matter."—Hannah

"True freedom comes from being under God's control and submitting to his authority—not from eating whatever I want whenever I want it."—Tracey

so carefully for so long, I thought I could no longer trust myself to make good decisions about what to eat and what not to eat. Because I did not trust myself to stop, for the past year I had simply never let myself have that first bite of anything "dangerous." It is ironic that I was so afraid of lacking self-control after I had demonstrated so much control for so long.

My eating disorder undermined my self-confidence. Because I had let myself develop such self-destructive habits, I no longer trusted my ability to make good decisions. I didn't realize how much I relied on my own good judgment about everyday activities until I lost that ability. When I ate a meal, I literally had no idea when to stop eating. For so long I had stopped eating too soon. Now I couldn't judge when I had eaten enough.

Because I had ignored my body's signals of when to eat, I could not depend on normal feelings of hunger and fullness. Normandi and Roark explain this phenomenon in their book *It's Not about Food*. They write, "Becoming aware of bodily sensations associated with eating is a special challenge for people with eating disorders. Many women have lost contact with the normal sensations and indicators of hunger, fullness, or feelings" (45). It was surprisingly difficult to get back in touch with my body and be able to make good decisions about food.

Ultimately, my recovery came down to trusting myself. As I began to get better and I experimented with letting go of my rigid control over my diet, I was gradually able to trust myself again. I thought the only way for me to be thin was through my own control. For a long time I was afraid that I would lose control and totally overeat, but as

Control

time went by, I saw that I wouldn't overeat and that I could learn appropriate moderation. As I let go of control, I was finally able to enjoy the freedom I had deprived myself of for so long. Letting go of control over my diet and my life was extremely liberating.

vanity

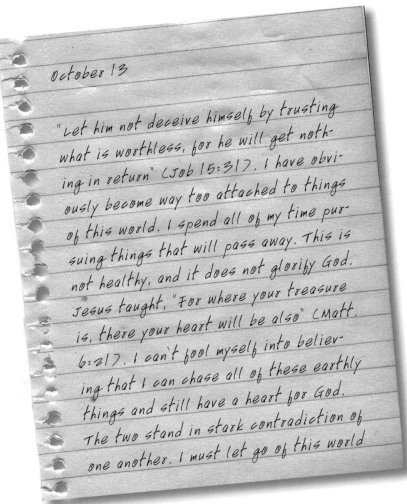

October 13

"Let him not deceive himself by trusting what is worthless, for he will get nothing in return" (Job 15:31). I have obviously become way too attached to things of this world. I spend all of my time pursuing things that will pass away. This is not healthy, and it does not glorify God. Jesus taught, "For where your treasure is, there your heart will be also" (Matt. 6:21). I can't fool myself into believing that I can chase all of these earthly things and still have a heart for God. The two stand in stark contradiction of one another. I must let go of this world *so that I can be free to love God fully. I am doing better in almost all aspects of my life, but I am still struggling with my fear of getting fat. This is just pure vanity. Until I overcome this, a large wall will stand between me and peace. I must truly let go of my vanity and my desire to be attractive. My worth and desirability are not based on my appearance but on my heart.*

I was embarrassed to admit to myself how vain I had become. Philippians 2:3 warns, "Do nothing out of selfish ambition or vain conceit." In the beginning, I had told myself I was only motivated by being in good shape, but by now I knew all I wanted was to be thin so that other people would find me attractive. I had never before thought of myself as vain. I never wore much makeup or put much time and energy into my appearance.

I believe my insecurities over being in a new, uncomfortable environment led me to become so concerned with being attractive. I was afraid people wouldn't like me. I thought I had to be thin to earn their acceptance. I wanted to feel liked and admired, and for me that feeling came with thinness. In my mind, to be beautiful was to be thin, and to be thin was to be liked.

We spend our time on what is important to us in life. Although I would have still said that God was my highest priority, I spent more time on my fitness than on anything else. I can't say that God was the center of my existence. Facing up to the reality of this was quite humbling. It showed me just how sad my life had become. I was finally starting to realize how pointless my anorexic lifestyle was.

No matter how hard I tried to fill my heart with satisfaction from thinness, I was always left feeling empty inside. Sure, I was proud of myself after a good workout or a healthy meal, but this feeling wouldn't last. Only one thing could fill my heart, and that was God. I tried to be filled with the passions of this world, and I came up short. Realizing that peace and comfort can come from God alone, I was now making my way back to God. If I wanted to be reconciled to God, I would need to let him help me deal with my vanity.

"I feel as though this is not something God can help me with mostly because my motivation is wrong. It's all about me and getting recognition from others and the joy of having my dad tell me I look good."—Jackie

"Sometimes I have that desire to look the best, and getting compliments on my looks becomes very important. So makeup and time spent preparing myself for the world to see me can sometimes be considered my idol."—Olivia

"Whenever I am around other girls I feel fat. I always feel like I'm the biggest one. I would like to lose weight in my thighs, hips, and stomach. If I did this I would be a lot more confident and a lot more comfortable. I also think it would help me with guys."—Nina

Vanity

10 Ways to Improve Body Image

1. Focus on personal attributes other than size, weight, or shape.
2. Minimize how much you talk about diet and weight.
3. Never joke about weight or size.
4. Examine your attitudes about weight and size. For example, do you treat people differently because of their weight?
5. Be aware of how our culture promotes thinness and don't buy into this mentality.
6. Try to recognize any distortions you may have about your body. Strive to see yourself realistically, acknowledging both strengths and weaknesses.
7. Be knowledgeable about resources for help. These include dietitians, psychologists, body image specialists, etc.
8. Do not diet or follow the latest weight-loss fads; instead develop a healthy lifestyle.
9. Don't equate thinness with happiness.
10. Remember that there is no "ideal" body. Beautiful bodies come in all sizes and shapes.

Adapted from the Renfrew Center, www.renfrewcenter.com

Selfishness

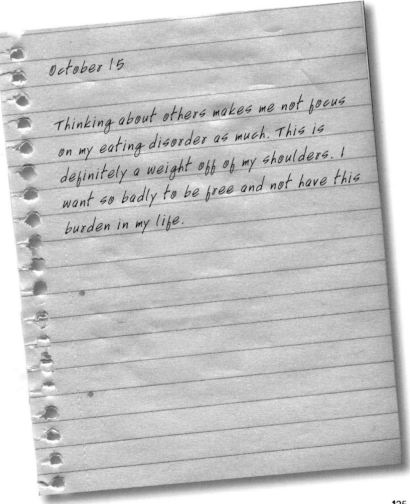

October 15

Thinking about others makes me not focus on my eating disorder as much. This is definitely a weight off of my shoulders. I want so badly to be free and not have this burden in my life.

When my problem

was at its worst, all I could think about was myself. Everything revolved around what I wanted or what I needed. Everything in my life had to fit in around my workouts and my unusual eating habits. A large part of my recovery process involved coming out from behind the wall I had built up around myself and starting to think about others again.

At first I thought about others to distract myself from my problem. Anything that could help me get my mind off of eating was a welcome change. But I was still motivated more by my own needs than by the needs of the people in my life. Once my thoughts and actions weren't so completely absorbed in concerns about my weight, I was able to see past myself and start to be a good friend again.

As I was able to change my focus, I remembered that God didn't want me to serve myself but to serve others. My obsessive-compulsive behavior was drawing my energy and atten-

"What made me move past this was the fact that I have a choice in the matter. I can choose to not be so obsessive and not so self-focused. It has helped to be busy and to have interests. It's important to have passions outside of yourself and to have goals and dreams and other things that keep you from being so self-indulgent."—Heather

tion away from serving others so that I was only living for myself. Not thinking about my weight all the time made me feel so free and liberated. Full of energy, I began to spend more time with my friends. I was once again able to listen to what was going on in their lives and genuinely care. Because of my self-destructive lifestyle, I really needed to look to God and others as a source of companionship, comfort, and joy.

Emotional Eating

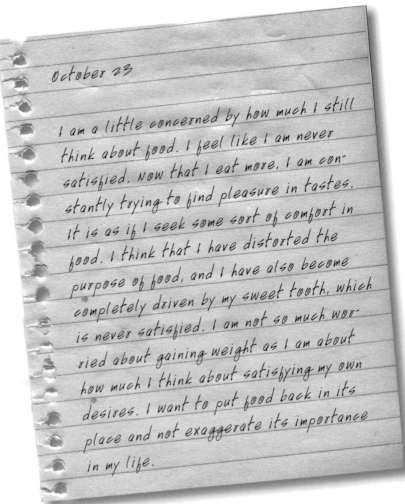

October 23

I am a little concerned by how much I still think about food. I feel like I am never satisfied. Now that I eat more, I am constantly trying to find pleasure in tastes. It is as if I seek some sort of comfort in food. I think that I have distorted the purpose of food, and I have also become completely driven by my sweet tooth, which is never satisfied. I am not so much worried about gaining weight as I am about how much I think about satisfying my own desires. I want to put food back in its place and not exaggerate its importance in my life.

People who struggle

with an eating disorder, whether it be overeating or undereating, are often searching for emotional satisfaction in food. This is what I meant when I wrote that I was seeking "some sort of comfort in food." We all have an empty feeling in our hearts that only God can fill. Unfortunately, we try to fill that void with all sorts of things, including food. This will only leave us feeling unsatisfied.

Although I was no longer avoiding food in order to feel good about myself, I needed something else to fill this void. Instead of not eating, I turned it around so that I would eat whenever I experienced this empty feeling. I think that this is why a lot of anorexics quickly gain extra weight back once they start to eat again. Instead of facing the emptiness in their hearts, they just fill it with something else. They replace not eating with overeating. Both are emotional coping mechanisms used to deal with other underlying pain.

"I fear food, but I love to eat. I abuse food at times by using it to comfort me when I'm down about something."—Whitney

"I eat when I'm nervous, then regret all I ate and don't even know how much I ate. I overeat to deal at times, but I also exercise way too much."—Laurie

"I find myself trying to fill myself with food instead of letting God meet those emotional needs."—Erin

Emotional Eating

Using food to cope with pain doesn't make the pain go away; it only numbs it for a while. Emotional eating also causes its own pain, such as feelings of guilt or low self-esteem. Romans 13:14 says, "Rather, clothe yourselves with the Lord Jesus Christ, and do not think about how to gratify the desires of the sinful nature." In my situation it was important for me to overeat during this time so that I could gain weight, but my attitude about food was still not right. I knew that it was wrong to seek emotional comfort in food.

Bad Habits

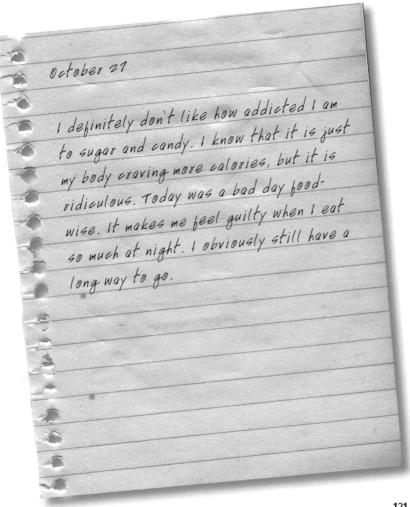

October 21

I definitely don't like how addicted I am to sugar and candy. I know that it is just my body craving more calories, but it is ridiculous. Today was a bad day food-wise. It makes me feel guilty when I eat so much at night. I obviously still have a long way to go.

Many girls who struggle with eating disorders eat sweets excessively. Because I deprived myself of normal food throughout the day, my blood sugar levels got so low that I craved sweet things packed with sugar. The sugar instantly satisfies the body's need for calories and also gives a sudden burst of energy. I would often still be hungry after completing my small dinners, so then the only alternative I left myself was to load up on fat-free desserts such as frozen yogurt. This is a typical behavior.

For example, I have seen girls who would have only spinach or carrots for dinner and then proceed to eat almost a whole batch of fat-free brownies for dessert. This type of eating habit is extremely unhealthy and is a good indication of disordered eating.

During my recovery, I would often eat the same small breakfast, lunch, and dinner that I was used to, but then in an effort to gain weight I would allow myself to eat large desserts. Even

"I need a bit more control over what I eat because I often eat too much junk. Eating is so fun, though. I love to exercise and I feel better afterward, but it just makes me hungrier and makes it harder to resist junk food."—Brandi

though I ended up gaining weight, I wish I had altered my diet in a more normal way. Adding to each meal would have been better than eating lots of sweets at night. A nutritionist should definitely be consulted to rebuild healthy eating habits rather than using this approach. Do not underestimate how difficult it is to recover natural eating habits after an eating disorder.

Although I needed the extra calories, I wish I hadn't gotten in the habit of snacking a lot after dinner. First of all, this usually meant I was eating alone, and there is nothing more lonely than standing in the kitchen having a mini-binge late at night when no one else is around. This is also a dangerous habit because it often leads to bulimia.

Although I never had extreme late-night binges and I never turned to bulimia, I always felt bad about myself when I was down in the kitchen alone. If I had eaten better meals when I was with my friends, I wouldn't have had to go for my late-night snack. I was just so afraid of food that when it came time to order, I always chose the salad. It was good that I allowed myself to eat more at night when I was hungry, but it only complicated my recovery. Eventually, I had to adjust this eating habit as well.

Rules

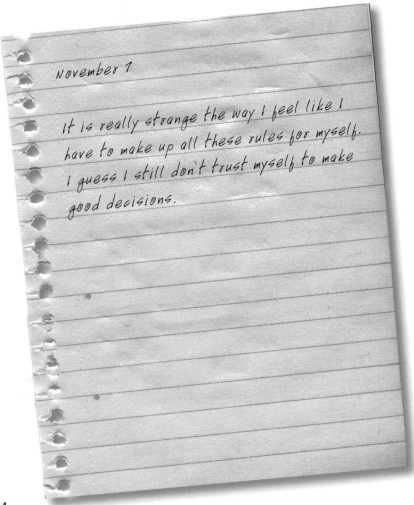

November 1

It is really strange the way I feel like I have to make up all these rules for myself. I guess I still don't trust myself to make good decisions.

Despite the progress

I had made, I was still in the habit of making rules for myself about eating. The diet mentality told me I had to have all kinds of rules to control my dangerous eating desires. This certainly is not true and can be damaging.

Some of my rules included: (1) sweets are only allowed after dinner, none during the day, and (2) eat only fruit as a snack between meals. I didn't trust myself to make good decisions about what I was going to eat, so I made rules for myself. My recovery process helped me let go of these rules, but whenever I was feeling out of control, I would reinstate one. I guess my rules were a security blanket for me. In my mind, they were my way of keeping my unruly desire for food in check.

I have learned from experience, though, that rules are not the way to maintain a healthy weight. The problem with these rules was that they disconnected me from my body's normal signals. My diet regulations taught

"I try not to pay attention to what I eat, but I often wish that I could be more disciplined in how much I eat at meals and snacks."—Erica

"I remember feeling as if I were trapped, in a sense, by the way I felt about my body and myself and the way I thought about other people."—Katy

me to ignore what my body was telling me and instead enforced the rules I had invented. God gave us the ability to sense when we are hungry, what types of food we are craving, and when we are full so that we will not need any rules. Because I was trying to control God's perfect creation, I had become unable to read my body's normal signals, which are a natural gift of God. I was no longer able to determine when I was and was not hungry, what I wanted to eat, or when I needed to stop eating. I had to relearn how to listen to my body and trust what it was telling me.

Now I am completely convinced that dieting simply does not work. It is one of the great myths of our culture. Those who try to diet typically either feel like failures and give up or become obsessed, as I did. It is virtually impossible, not to mention extremely unhealthy, to deny the basic human need for food for an extended period of time.

Coping Mechanisms

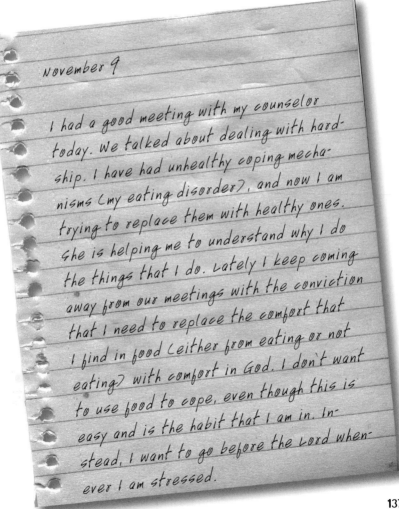

November 9

I had a good meeting with my counselor today. We talked about dealing with hardship. I have had unhealthy coping mechanisms (my eating disorder), and now I am trying to replace them with healthy ones. She is helping me to understand why I do the things that I do. Lately I keep coming away from our meetings with the conviction that I need to replace the comfort that I find in food (either from eating or not eating) with comfort in God. I don't want to use food to cope, even though this is easy and is the habit that I am in. Instead, I want to go before the Lord whenever I am stressed.

I was comforted by the fact that now my counselor and I could come up with specific things I could do to change my habits. At first we had talked about everything in such general terms that I would get frustrated. Now I had certain things to work on each week. Because I had a plan of action, I was hopeful that I could fix my bad habits. Over the past year, I had dealt with my pain by seeking satisfaction in my skinniness. If I felt down, a good workout or having just a salad for dinner would make me feel better. Or even better, stepping on the scale and seeing that I had lost another pound would really make me feel good. Any pain that I might experience would be numbed by my new coping mechanism. When my counselor and I discovered how I had developed this habit, it was a significant breakthrough.

Seeking comfort in food has been a difficult habit to break. Even now I struggle with wanting to get on the scale and see that I have lost weight. It's dif-

"Breaking up with my boyfriend, along with the stress of school, contributed to my overeating and were the biggest preceding factors of my struggles. I have not had a boyfriend since then, and I began to gain weight—each year it seems to get worse."—Lucie

"I feel a void of loneliness that I try to fill with food. Since I don't have the pleasure of hanging out with a boy or being excited about someone, I eat because I enjoy eating and it makes me feel better short-term."—Carey

"I was just so lonely and tried to find a new identity in being thin."—Kaitlyn

"When I was in a relationship, I felt beautiful and satisfied and complete and never thought about eating when I wasn't hungry. I like food, but I had a reason to stop eating because I wanted to hang out with my boyfriend and I wanted to stay looking good for him. Now I don't have someone's hand to hold or someone to look cute for, so I turn to food instead."—Kimberly

ficult to stop seeing weight loss as an indication that I have been working hard. During my recovery, putting on clothes that made me look really skinny also made me feel good about myself. On the other hand, I would want to eat a huge bowl of ice cream or some other comfort food whenever I got bored or lonely. These are all ways I would use food as an emotional crutch.

Realizing that I used food for comfort showed me that I needed to develop new coping mechanisms. During this transition I was in a particularly vulnerable emotional state. I had no defense because I couldn't let myself use my old habit of not eating and I hadn't yet developed a new, healthy form of coping. When I got upset, I would usually get *really* upset, not knowing where to turn.

The first thing my counselor and I decided was that I needed to stop and take a deep breath whenever I felt my emotions or thoughts getting out of control. Then I would say a prayer and ask God to help me. For example, I prayed according to Psalm 32:7: "You are my hiding place; you will protect me from trouble and surround me with songs of deliverance." Everyone has coping mechanisms, and of all of the strategies I have tried, none is as effective as depending on God.

Discovering how I used my eating disorder to cope was one of the many ways that I benefited from professional help. I don't think I would have come to this conclusion on my own. Although my counselor would never give me direct answers, she guided me toward understanding things for myself. With this prompting, I was able to learn much about myself on my own, which was an empowering experience.

I believe that my work with my counselor was successful because I spent so much time thinking about our sessions when we weren't together. In other words, I did my homework. Because I was serious about our work together and I truly tried to apply the things we talked about to my life, my recovery actually proceeded quite rapidly. My counseling was of great benefit because I was willing to put in the effort to address my problem. I took seriously verses such as Proverbs 15:32, which says, "He who ignores discipline despises himself, but whoever heeds correction gains understanding."

In the sessions with my counselor, I was able to talk openly about God. Although we never discussed her faith and she was not a Christian counselor, she respected my faith and accepted that it could help me with my problem. I'm not sure what other counselors are like, but I think I was fortunate in how mine handled my faith. However, I think that if I'd had the opportunity to go to a Christian counselor, that would have been better for me, and I would strongly suggest this whenever possible.

How Does God Fit In?

As I explored the underlying issues of my eating disorder, I wrestled with how God fit into everything I was going through. I didn't understand how this could have happened to me since I was a Christian when I started down this slippery slope of disordered eating and exercise habits and I remained dedicated to God throughout this time in my life. How could I develop such idols in my life when I was really trying to live for God? Despite the challenge of working through these issues, my relationship with God was what ultimately empowered me to fight my way back to health and recovery. This struggle actually helped me to grow in my faith in a way that I do not think I would have been able to otherwise. In the following pages I address the question, How does God fit in?

Gaining Perspective

November 26

Thanksgiving Day. We saw a news special on feeding the hungry and homeless today, and it reminded me how much I have to be thankful for and how much I have taken for granted. The fact that I would spend so much of my time and energy worrying about food is sickening to me. I definitely take myself way too seriously, and I think that if I had more of a thankful heart, then I wouldn't be so preoccupied with myself. I think I have made good progress this fall, but I still have a ways to go.

Thanksgiving break

was a distinct turning point in my recovery. From when I returned to school in late August until Thanksgiving break, all I did was maintain my weight. This time with my family reinforced that I was too thin and that I truly needed to gain weight. After this break I committed myself to eating more, and I finally began to gain back some of the weight I had lost over the past year. There were many things about this time with my family that enabled me to make this positive step forward.

Seeing a television special on the hungry, for example, opened my eyes to the fact that while thousands of people were going hungry in this country, I was intentionally starving myself. This was like a slap in the face, showing me how poorly I had been treating myself and how much I had been taking for granted. Realizing how little food some people have, made me see that I needed to appreciate what I have.

"I have started to look at exercise as a way to relieve stress and be good to my body. When I am doing it excessively, it is neither of these things. It's not stress-relieving because it takes up too much time, and it's not good for my body because it's too much abuse. I started to think about the serious repercussions of my actions and how selfish it was to think so much about my own body and my own appearance."—Corrie

"Being around others who are more consumed with these things than I am shows me how incredibly self-centered of a lifestyle it is. It totally turns me off. In a sense, that is a good thing—to have that perspective—because it makes me want to be nothing like it!"—Jessica

Reach Out by Letting Others Help You

1. Seek professional counseling. A mental health professional will help you develop a healthy social support network that will include all of the following items.
2. Meet with a nutritionist. A nutritionist can help you develop a healthy eating plan that is designed specifically for you (reading nutrition articles in magazines or on the Internet will not help in the same personalized way as meeting with a professional).
3. See a doctor. Having a complete physical will help you identify any health issues that you may be experiencing as a result of food and exercise struggles.
4. Get plugged into your church. Being involved in your Christian community is vital and will help you develop the following areas on this list.
5. Have an accountability partner. Find a trustworthy peer who you can meet with regularly to discuss what God is doing in your life. This is someone that will both encourage and challenge you.
6. Find a mentor. We all need someone who is a step ahead of us in life to support us. This is someone that you can ask tough questions and learn from their experiences.
7. Join a small group. A Bible study or small group can offer support, prayer, truth, and encouragement. Hearing other people's struggles can help put yours into perspective.
8. Serve others. Find people who you can serve, such as someone younger you can mentor or social work you can be involved in. Pouring yourself into others will help put your own struggles into perspective.

So much of my struggle during my anorexia had to do with my perspective. I've always had virtually anything I ever wanted. It was as if I had to *create* a problem for myself. Having to deal with my eating disorder seemed like such a difficult struggle to me; meanwhile, people across the country were homeless or battling cancer or mourning the loss of a loved

Gaining Perspective

one. It was embarrassing how petty my problem seemed in comparison to the challenges other people face. This perspective allowed me to see how much of my problem I had created in my own mind. And if I had created it, then I also had the power to tear it down.

"From everyone who has been given much, much will be demanded; and from the one who has been entrusted with much, much more will be asked" (Luke 12:48). I knew that the Lord wanted so much more from me than I was giving. God had richly blessed me, and I needed to adjust my attitude so that I could make the most of all that he had given me.

Spending quality time with my family also helped motivate me to continue to recover. I am very close to my brother, and he was the first one to suggest that perhaps I was just taking myself too seriously. He told me that no one who loved me cared about how skinny I was. Somehow this seemed profound to me. I had become obsessed with my weight because I wanted to be loved and accepted, but I was already loved no matter what I looked like. It was helpful for me to be surrounded by the unconditional love of my family during this vulnerable time in my life.

These significant discoveries allowed me to recognize the error in my thinking. In the past three months I had begun to better understand my problem so that I could realize when I was being irrational. I was taking important steps in identifying my weaknesses. Admitting the sin in my life was challenging, but now it was time to go back to school and make some changes. I returned from that Thanksgiving vacation with a new resolve to continue on my road to recovery.

Worldliness

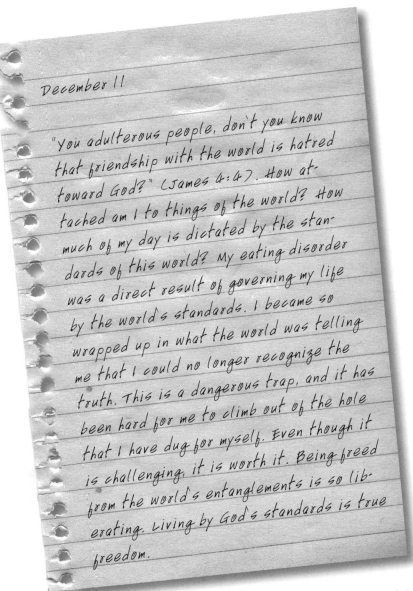

December 11

"You adulterous people, don't you know that friendship with the world is hatred toward God?" (James 4:4). How attached am I to things of the world? How much of my day is dictated by the standards of this world? My eating disorder was a direct result of governing my life by the world's standards. I became so wrapped up in what the world was telling me that I could no longer recognize the truth. This is a dangerous trap, and it has been hard for me to climb out of the hole that I have dug for myself. Even though it is challenging, it is worth it. Being freed from the world's entanglements is so liberating. Living by God's standards is true freedom.

Every day we face the messages the media want us to believe. Girls are overwhelmed with pictures of supermodels—supposedly the most attractive women in the world—who look like skeletons. Fat-free foods are all over the grocery stores and are constantly promoted as the healthy alternative. The number of quick-fix diets is steadily increasing. As a woman in my twenties, I found it virtually impossible to ignore these messages about body image.

The Bible leaves no doubt about the need to separate from the world. Being in the world but not of the world can have various meanings, but for me it meant living in the middle of all the weight propaganda and not letting myself obsess over my body. My concern with my weight was clearly a worldly concern, but once I was caught in the media's web—believing all of its lies—I found it difficult to escape.

During this time, I believed the lie that I could never be too thin—that the skinnier I was, the

"Feeling the pressure from the world, as well as competition with other girls, contributes to my desire to be smaller, which fuels the desire to exercise more. I also think that Americans, as a whole, are self-indulgent and self-absorbed, and so it is hard to not buy into that."—Victoria

"Looking at fashion and health magazines like *Shape* or *InStyle* negatively impacts my body image. I have to guard myself from indulging in magazines like that because it is so easy to think that if I do not look like these women, then my body is unattractive or in some way wrong. If I know looking at *Shape* and *Vogue* are hard for me, then I need to set boundaries to not look at those magazines."—Nancy

"I need to be more concerned with inner beauty and pleasing God than with myself and outer beauty, which the world values."—Renee

more attractive I was. I also believed that I had to work out every day or I would get fat. I thought that if I didn't eat fat-free foods, I wasn't taking care of my body. In my mind, fat was the enemy and should be avoided at all costs. I thought I should always be on some sort of diet. I believed I couldn't trust my body's normal signs of hunger and satisfaction. I believed the lie that I should control everything I eat. I thought women shouldn't eat very much. I was seeking fulfillment in all these lies.

I hadn't heeded Paul's warning in Romans 1:25: "They exchanged the truth of God for a lie, and worshiped and served created things rather than the Creator—who is forever praised." I was living in sin and not according to God's truth. To find my way back to God, I had to have a firm foundation of his truth. John 8:32 says, "Then you will know the truth, and the truth will set you free." It was important for me to be in constant communication with God and to study his Word daily so that I would know the truth. Although the challenges I faced may be different from the challenges the people of biblical times faced, the theme is still the same. The stories in the Bible describe people who were struggling, just as I was, not to give in to the world's standards.

I think I was especially susceptible to the world's lies during this time because I was reading the Bible but not really listening to what it was saying. I did not want to see how closely the stories applied to my life. I was afraid to confront the clear truth of the Bible.

Spiritual Warfare

December 16

"For in my inner being I delight in God's law; but I see another law at work in the members of my body, waging war against the law of my mind and making me a prisoner of the law of sin at work within my members. What a wretched man I am! Who will rescue me from this body of death? Thanks be to God—through Jesus Christ our Lord!" (Rom. 7:22-25). This is exactly how I have felt about my eating disorder. I always got so frustrated with myself for this sin in my life, but how comforting it is to know that others have struggled in exactly the same way that I have.

When I read this Bible verse from Romans, I was struck by how well it described what I had been feeling. Paul expressed my struggles and my pain. Throughout my eating disorder I felt a war waging within me. On the one hand, I had a desire to pursue thinness at all costs. On the other hand, my rational mind told me how ridiculous this was. I fought my physical form while my spiritual self told me I was not glorifying God with my actions. These two sides battled back and forth in my mind, each wanting to control my thoughts and actions.

Although some people prefer not to talk about Satan or evil, through my experiences with my eating disorder I have come to believe that spiritual warfare is a very real thing. I believe in the struggle between good and evil and that this struggle exists within each of us. My relationship with God was good and pure until it became tainted with deceitful messages and self-destructive thoughts.

"We let food control our life, and ultimately it interferes with our focus and relationship with God. May I glorify God through the physical body that he has blessed me with. I don't want to let food and body image consume my life."—Marjorie

"I think that so much of my negative body image or desire to be skinny is the work of the devil. It is a bad spirit telling me I need to conform to the ways of the world, and that is not how God sees us."—Ali

"The enemy was telling me lies and trying to make me believe they were true. These were lies about my own body: 'You're so fat. You're unattractive and unlikable.' I praise God that eventually I was able to see that these are all lies and that our Creator does not want his creation to think in such ways."—Sterling

Spiritual Warfare

Despite the power of these evil, damaging forces in my life, God never left my side. Psalm 23:4 says, "Even though I walk through the valley of the shadow of death, I will fear no evil, for you are with me." If God had left me, I would have been defeated; I couldn't overcome this evil on my own. Instead, God was always there in the back of my mind whispering that what I was doing was wrong. God was persistent enough that I eventually recognized the sin in my life.

When Paul cries out, "What a wretched man I am!" I can certainly relate. There were times when I was absolutely disgusted with myself. I saw how horrible my thoughts had become and how obsessed with myself I was. I felt like I could not escape my sin. Looking back, I realize how valuable it was for me to see the worst side of myself. It was such a humbling experience. Because I had never been broken like that before, I had never really been able to understand my own sinfulness. Like Paul, I recognized the sick state of my own soul, and it drew me to God.

Seeing the Good

December 19

It is good to be home. It is even better to be home and be happy and healthy. I am myself again. I don't know where I went or why I left, but I am home in so many ways. I have been through a lot this fall, and every step of the way God has been by my side. Having an eating disorder has been a true blessing. Even though it has been a real trial, I have learned so much about God through it. I feel that I am a much stronger person now, and having seen what a support the Lord has been has really strengthened my faith in his providence. Although hard times are never fun, God uses them to mold us into the servants that he wants us to be.

Not until I left home did I realize what it truly means to be "at home." My home was so much more than where I lived and grew up. My home was a place where I was safe. It was a place where I always knew I was loved. I felt comfortable there; I could really be myself. There were no conditions that I had to meet or expectations that I had to fill to be welcome. It was my sanctuary.

When I left for college, I had to say good-bye to that home. I maintained my relationships, and my family supported me even though I was far away, but so much of my life was new. I felt uncomfortable and uneasy much of the time. But never once in my entire freshman year of college did I ever let myself cry because I was homesick. I was so anxious to show my independence that I ignored my pain and loneliness. To deal with the emptiness in my heart, I threw myself into my work, especially my work on my fitness. My body became my project—my way to divert my attention from my loss of home.

"My faith is the only thing that has sustained me through such bouts of insecurity and self-doubt. I know that the Lord never gives you more than you can handle and that every struggle is his way of pruning you so that you may bear more fruit. Knowing that he loves me that much and wants to see me flourish is essential."—Eliza

My problem was made worse because of my spiritual weakness. Away from my home, I didn't realize that the true home of my heart is with God. He was with me in this new place, but I didn't recognize it. If I had admitted that I was sad and homesick, I think I would have found comfort in God's presence. Instead, I ignored my loneliness and turned away from God. Because I was not honest with myself, I couldn't be real with God either.

My desire to be strong and independent actually made me weaker than ever. I sought to assert my emotional strength by becoming physically strong instead. I sought physical endurance as a substitute for emotional endurance. I thought I could prove to everyone how well I was doing if I was thin and fit. I thought my body could be a symbol of my strength and well-being. I hid behind my fitness so that I wouldn't have to deal with my homesickness.

Eventually, though, I found my way home. Going home to Houston for Christmas break that year was such a wonderful experience. Not only was I with my family again, but I was healing both physically and spiritually. I was starting to feel comfortable with myself again. For the first time since I admitted my anorexia, I felt like the worst was over.

Now that I was past the worst of my struggle, I was beginning to see all the good that was coming out of my trial. When I was in the midst of the battle, all I wanted was to be rescued. By this point, I could see how much everything I had been through had helped me become a stronger person. It is often difficult to understand why God lets bad things happen, but his vision is much larger than ours. I was able to find peace with my eating disorder when I trusted in his perfect plan for my life.

What It Means to Be a Woman

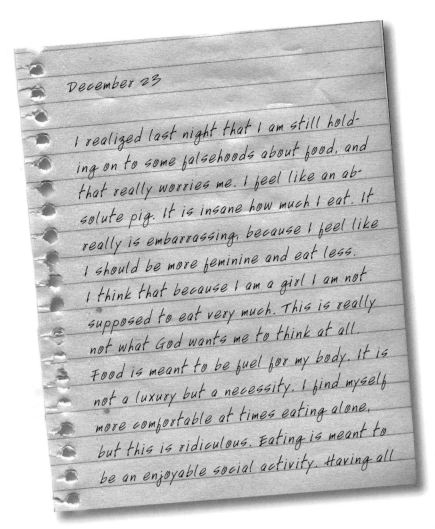

December 23

I realized last night that I am still holding on to some falsehoods about food, and that really worries me. I feel like an absolute pig. It is insane how much I eat. It really is embarrassing, because I feel like I should be more feminine and eat less. I think that because I am a girl I am not supposed to eat very much. This is really not what God wants me to think at all. Food is meant to be fuel for my body. It is not a luxury but a necessity. I find myself more comfortable at times eating alone, but this is ridiculous. Eating is meant to be an enjoyable social activity. Having all

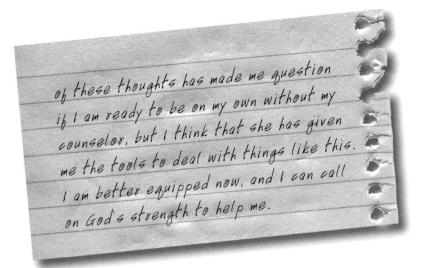

of these thoughts has made me question if I am ready to be on my own without my counselor, but I think that she has given me the tools to deal with things like this. I am better equipped now, and I can call on God's strength to help me.

Increasing the quantity of food I ate made me realize how much I had come to associate femininity with eating small amounts of food. To be a woman, I thought, was to be dainty and to have a small appetite. As I researched more about anorexia, I realized that this mentality contributes to the epidemic. I have come to learn that this idea is held by many women, and actually began as early as the Victorian period.

Growing up as a female athlete, I was always sensitive about asserting my femininity. I often wore skirts to school and liked keeping my hair long. I didn't want to be mistaken for a boyish female athlete. At some point during college, I began to associate being skinny and eating very little with femininity as well. I think I wanted to feel like a woman, and not eating much gave me that feeling. The irony was that eating so little made my body look like I was a twelve-year-old boy, with no curves or shape whatsoever—hardly the figure of a maturing woman.

I guess I learned my habits from my friends. All of my friends at school who were thin and attractive didn't eat much. So many female athletes appear masculine, and I didn't want to have that image. I thought women were supposed to eat salads and just pick at their food. Because I thought this, I gradually became embarrassed about eating.

Once I linked eating small amounts of food with being womanly, I was embarrassed to eat a lot. This embarrassment made me want to eat alone, which was not good. My embarrassment also rendered me unable to confess to others when I was hungry, especially if they were not. I wanted to deny my appetite altogether.

The girls I spent time with in college seemed to be constantly talking about what they did or did not eat, always battling their appetites. Marya Hornbacher wrote about this experience in her own life: "We talked about weight nonstop, about how much we wanted to lose, asked each other: Do I look like I gained weight? Lost weight?

"I am self-conscious about my body, but I try to overcome this by saying that I need to be this way for my sport and that others just think I'm strong, not fat. But I'm almost always aware of it or try to cover up areas I don't like."—Mary

"I think it is important to surround yourself with women who have a healthy perspective. This doesn't mean women who never exercise or eat only junk. I think it's important to have a healthy lifestyle, but there should be room for being flexible and not being controlled by these things."—Emily

"My experience in college was unlike most of my friends' experiences because that is when I least struggled with these issues. I watched my friends exercise excessively, eat broccoli and ketchup for dinner, wither away to nothing, and refuse to believe anything was wrong. But in the back of my mind I was asking myself if this was the reason they were getting asked out more."—Helen

[Do I] look big in this skirt, in these jeans, when I stand like this?" (104–5). She then describes why girls spend so much time talking about food and what they ate: because they are often hungry from not letting themselves eat enough. When people are trying to control their appetites, they can't help but think about and talk about food. So it becomes a constant battle as women struggle to block out their appetites but are only more and more controlled by food.

Accepting Myself

December 21

I don't feel like I am an accepting person, and I think it starts with the fact that I am not accepting of myself. I am hard on myself in many different facets of my life. It is hard for me to forgive myself for mistakes, especially when they are mistakes that I think I should have been able to prevent. I have this standard that I set for myself, and then I don't accept anything less. This tendency could easily be seen in my eating disorder. I was horrible to myself. Then because I am so judgmental of myself, I apply these standards to everyone else. After all, shouldn't they have to work as hard as I have been? Being on vacation with my family has shown me how truly unaccepting I am. I am most critical of the things that I don't allow myself to do. For example, my dad's poor eating habits drive me crazy, since I am trying so hard to control my own eating. This is a horrible habit that I have developed that needs to be addressed and corrected. I find it interfering with my relationships. I need to learn to love myself as God loves me, fully and unconditionally. In order to love your neighbor as yourself, you must first love yourself. I am not talking about pride or self-absorption. I am just talking about being comfortable with myself.

During this time, how I was relating to others was determined by how I related to myself. On my family's Christmas vacation, I realized what a problem it had become. My dad, whom I absolutely adore, is a bit overweight. He doesn't get to exercise much, and he eats basically whatever he wants. On this vacation I found myself being severely critical of him. It drove me crazy to watch him eat fattening foods like cheeseburgers and french fries. My obsession was once again coming between me and the people I love the most. When I realized what I was doing, I was horrified. My dad had been so generous to take the family on vacation, and yet I didn't want him to enjoy himself.

The real problem in this situation was how I was treating myself. Because I actually wanted to let my guard down and let myself enjoy food, it made me angry when I saw others do it. I hated that they could let themselves enjoy food when all I could think about was the calories. I longed to have a healthy, positive relationship with food again. Instead, I just felt bitter toward those who could actually enjoy mealtime.

As you can see, my eating disorder affected my relationships in many different ways. Because I was so harsh with myself, I became harsh with others. My problem had driven a wedge between me and the people I love the most. Looking back on it now, it hurts me to see how self-destructive my eating disorder really was. Its effects reached

"I need to stop looking for people's responses to make me feel pretty or good about myself. I need to stop worrying all the time about what I look like and just be confident in myself."—Anna

"I'd like to be like those huge ladies on talk shows who say that they are totally confident about what their body looks like, even though it's against society's norms."—Ginger

"I have resigned myself to accepting how God has made me. Though I'm not always happy about how I look, I think that is just the way it is and I should just deal with it and move on."—Tricia

so far into my life. It was good for me to be able to make the connection between my critical attitude toward others and my eating disorder. This enabled me to see how truly important it was for me to recover fully. I didn't want my problem to continue to damage all my relationships.

Filled by God

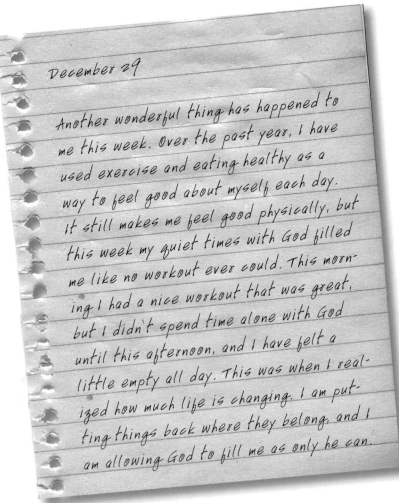

December 29

Another wonderful thing has happened to me this week. Over the past year, I have used exercise and eating healthy as a way to feel good about myself each day. It still makes me feel good physically, but this week my quiet times with God filled me like no workout ever could. This morning I had a nice workout that was great, but I didn't spend time alone with God until this afternoon, and I have felt a little empty all day. This was when I realized how much life is changing. I am putting things back where they belong, and I am allowing God to fill me as only he can.

I had tried to fill my life with so many different things. I tried to fill it with the adrenaline of working out or the satisfaction of eating healthy. But as 1 Timothy 4:8 says, "For physical training is of some value, but godliness has value for all things, holding promise for both the present life and the life to come." As a result of my struggles, I have realized that my desire to be loved can only be filled by sharing my life with God. I tried to satisfy this desire with other things, and while they may have brought temporary satisfaction, nothing could remotely offer the eternal satisfaction that God does.

Before I devoted my life to God during high school, I put all my energy into succeeding—succeeding in school, succeeding in tennis. My goal in life was to be the best I could be at everything I did. My self-esteem came from my accomplishments. I also drew a great deal of my self-worth

"Spiritually I think I should think about my body as being God's temple and I should treat it accordingly."—Brittany

"I've had trouble with identity when I wasn't improving in my sport. My happiness was dependent on how I did. However, God brought me through it. I gained joy in my salvation and strength and hope."—Lizzy

from my relationships with my family and friends. This life was satisfying for me until the day it all came crashing down. In high school, when I experienced the worst tennis loss of my career, I realized how empty my life really was. Without my success, nothing seemed to have any meaning. This was when I turned to God. I finally realized the truth that Lisa Bevere eloquently expresses when she writes, "The true measure of a woman does not lie in the number of her God-given talents and abilities, but in her faithfulness to use them to honor her master" (62). I had spent my time seeking my own glory, not his.

It was so refreshing to realize I had a true purpose in life that wouldn't shatter the way my search for success had. I realized that loving God and being loved by him gave real meaning to my existence. I suddenly had a new perspective on what was important in my life. "What is more, I consider everything a loss compared to the surpassing greatness of knowing Christ Jesus my Lord, for whose sake I have lost all things" (Phil. 3:8).

The first time I turned to God after pursuing the world's glory was a result of my weakness. The second time I turned to God after trying to live by the standards of the world was once again a result of my weakness. After giving my life to God in high school, I strayed from him because I wanted to be loved by the world—I wanted to be skinny, to be beautiful, to feel attractive. I left his loving arms, seeking security in the praise of men. When I finally faced my sin, I returned to God, weak and desperate. When I tried to please the world, I only found destruction.

My workouts could give me a temporary feeling of satisfaction, but spending good time alone with God gave me lasting peace. Life lived from one workout to the next was a life without peace. I had built a wall between myself and God, but now I was able to break through that wall. Being at peace with God again was the crucial step on my road to recovery.

Trusting

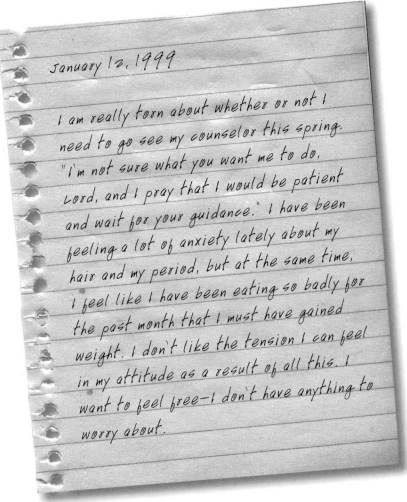

January 12, 1999

I am really torn about whether or not I need to go see my counselor this spring. "I'm not sure what you want me to do, Lord, and I pray that I would be patient and wait for your guidance." I have been feeling a lot of anxiety lately about my hair and my period, but at the same time, I feel like I have been eating so badly for the past month that I must have gained weight. I don't like the tension I can feel in my attitude as a result of all this. I want to feel free—I don't have anything to worry about.

Even with as much as I had learned and improved over the past semester, there were still times when I would get tremendously anxious about my weight. Over Christmas break I experienced a wide variety of emotions. During this time I was thinking a lot about whether I was ready to stop seeing my counselor. The concern I still had about my weight made me doubt my earlier feeling that our work was done. I wanted to be on my own, but I did not want to stop too soon and prevent a full recovery.

At times over the break I felt like I was still way too thin (which, by the way, I certainly was). *Two common side effects of having an eating disorder are thinning of hair because of a lack of protein and not being able to have a normal period because of a lack of body fat.* I was experiencing both of these symptoms. Although I had already gained back some of the weight I had lost, it takes a long time for hair to become strong again and for your body to start menstruating

"I would like to continue to build my self-esteem and my view of myself. When I put everything in God's control, he will build my self-esteem, which will continue to allow me to not look at my body so negatively."—Heather

regularly. I knew it would take more time, but I was anxious for these problems to go away. I resented how they reminded me of my self-destructive behavior. Both symptoms were important signs that I was not giving my body what it needed to function. This made me determined to gain more weight.

Looking at old pictures of myself was also quite troublesome for me. When I saw how much heavier I used to be, I was afraid that if I started eating normally again, I would return to that size. I was torn between my desire to recover from my eating disorder and my desire to remain thin. I didn't want the problem, but I didn't want to let go of the thinness either.

Having all of this on my mind made me tense most of the time. I was constantly struggling with a mix of all of these emotions. Plus, I was trying to be honest with myself about whether or not I needed to go back to my counselor. It was good that I had Christmas break to think about all this and reflect on how I was doing. Being at home and having some time to myself was therapeutic. I had made excellent progress over the fall, and I wanted to continue to improve.

After not being honest with myself for so long, I was worried that I couldn't trust my judgment. I wanted to do the right thing about my therapy. I had felt pretty sure about it when I left school, but now that I was feeling concerned about my weight again, I wondered if I was just fooling myself. Was I ready to be on my own? Had I improved, or was I still just ignoring my problem? I felt I could no longer trust my own decisions. I am so thankful I had God leading me in my decision, because I certainly never could have gotten through this on my own.

Healing

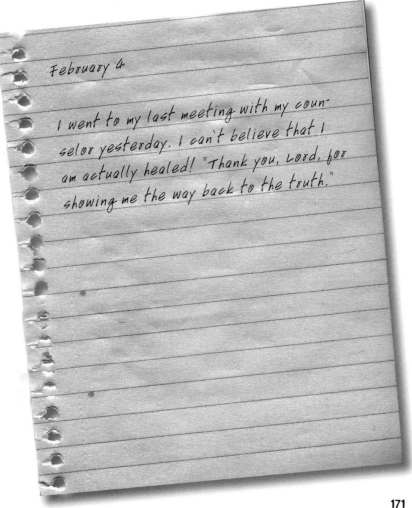

February 4

I went to my last meeting with my counselor yesterday. I can't believe that I
am actually healed! "Thank you, Lord, for
showing me the way back to the truth."

Being finished with my work with the counselor was certainly liberating. Although I wrote in my journal that I was healed, I still needed to work through many things. I wanted to be better so badly that many times I thought I was. Unfortunately, I would go back to my bad habits soon after that. Looking back, I do think I was ready to stop meeting with my counselor, but not because I was completely free of my eating disorder.

Meeting with the counselor each week gave me the tools to understand and fight my problem. Unfortunately, one person can do only so much to help another. Ultimately, healing has to come from inside and from God. My counselor taught me so much. Our conversations enabled me to explore several different factors that contributed to the development of my anorexia. Because of everything my counselor taught me, I was able to discover on my own even more of the factors that had af-

"It has really helped me that I have been in a healthy relationship with someone who genuinely loves me no matter what I look like. . . . The way he loves me reminds me every day of how God loves me. And God loves me a thousand times more."—Michelle

"God has given me a desire to help other women and fight for them by relating to them and also by listening and understanding their hearts."—Paula

fected me. I think it was good for me to stop seeing my counselor at this time, because it would have been harmful for me to depend on her too much.

I originally hesitated to get help at all, because I thought I should be able to solve my problem with the help of God alone. I now believe God sent my counselor into my life to help me begin to get back on the right path. My counselor challenged me and helped me battle back when I couldn't have done it alone. God works in and through other people all the time, and I am grateful to my counselor for her help. There came a time, however, when I needed to deal with some things on my own, just between God and me. He let me know it was time.

The world of psychology and the world of religion often have a lot of conflict between them. I study both fields, so I see this conflict often in my work. Although I believe God was my greatest source of support, I do think there was a place for professional help in my recovery. Some Christians think counselors can't be trusted, but it's not fair to underestimate their ability to help. It's important, of course, to always listen to counselors in light of the truth of God. In my counseling it was as if I had to filter the advice through the teachings of the Bible. Even though my counselor was not a Christian counselor, I think God was at the center of our interactions. He was with us in each of our meetings, because he was present in my heart. I believe God knew I was having trouble hearing him on my own, so he worked through my counselor to show me the truth.

Where Do I Go from Here?

Part 5

My work with my counselor helped me learn how to identify the problems I was struggling with and explore the issues that lay beneath the surface. Although I made the decision that I was ready to be on my own and that I no longer needed to see my counselor weekly, this was certainly not the end of my recovery story. Recovery was a process that would continue for years to come as I sought more self-awareness and growth. My counselor was crucial in equipping me to do this work, but now it was time for me to continue the work on my own. During this next step, I had to apply the skills that I had acquired in counseling and ask myself the question, Where do I go from here?

Continual Work

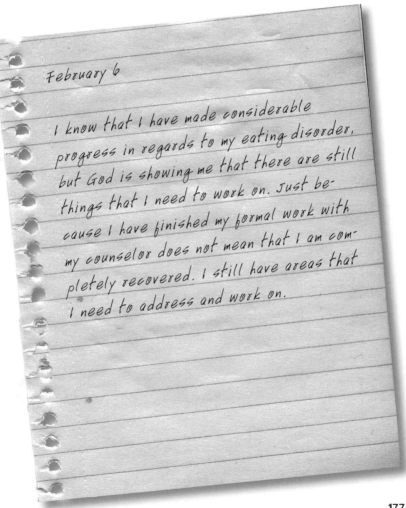

February 6

I know that I have made considerable progress in regards to my eating disorder, but God is showing me that there are still things that I need to work on. Just because I have finished my formal work with my counselor does not mean that I am completely recovered. I still have areas that I need to address and work on.

It was humbling for me to realize I was not yet fully recovered. From the first day I set my heart on recovery, all I wanted to do was get better. I set my eyes on the goal, and I would not let myself see anything else. Whenever I had a setback, I would get frustrated and disappointed with myself. By now this had happened often enough that I was used to it. Verses such as Philippians 3:12 expressed my heart: "Not that I have already obtained all this, or have already been made perfect, but I press on to take hold of that for which Christ Jesus took hold of me." Because I was no longer seeing my counselor, I was learning to turn to God for help. I trusted that he was my source of strength and guidance, and I knew I wasn't alone in my struggle. This verse comforted me: "I lift up my eyes to the hills—where does my help come from? My help comes from the LORD, the Maker of heaven and earth" (Ps. 121:1–2).

Life is a continual process of growth, development, and learn-

"I should exercise regularly and eat healthy (and do this joyfully) because my body is a temple and God's dwelling place. I should keep it fit for a King."—Sandy

"I find it helpful to write out on note cards verses about body image and how we are called to view ourselves."—Leslie

ing. Each day I seemed to learn something new about my eating disorder or discover an area of my life that still needed work. God describes his children as clay that he is constantly shaping and molding into his pottery. I found this to be especially true with how he used my eating disorder to make me into the person he wanted me to be.

I am glad I didn't fool myself into thinking I was recovered simply because my counselor and I had decided we didn't need to meet anymore. It would have been easy to deceive myself into believing I didn't need to deal with that area of my life anymore. If I had been content with where I was, my eating disorder might have eventually returned again. I didn't want my anorexia to ever come back, so I would catch myself at the slightest sign of my old habits. I needed a lot of discipline to keep going in my efforts toward a full recovery once I didn't have my counselor's weekly help. I had to be aware of my thoughts and extremely honest with myself about what was going on.

Stepping Outside
Of Myself

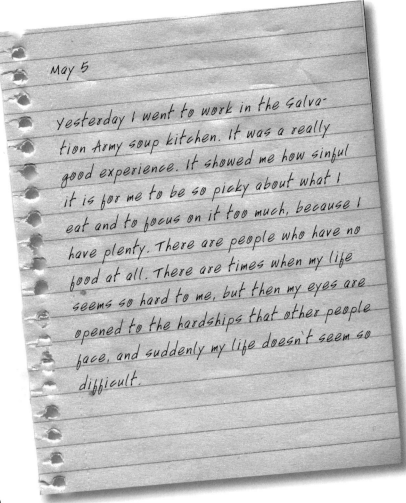

May 5

Yesterday I went to work in the Salvation Army soup kitchen. It was a really good experience. It showed me how sinful it is for me to be so picky about what I eat and to focus on it too much, because I have plenty. There are people who have no food at all. There are times when my life seems so hard to me, but then my eyes are opened to the hardships that other people face, and suddenly my life doesn't seem so difficult.

My **experience** at the Salvation Army soup kitchen was similar to seeing the hunger special on TV over Thanksgiving. It's always good to see things from other people's perspective. God wanted me to see those people and to become more grateful for what he has given me. Most of the people at the soup kitchen were homeless. Left with nothing, they were forced to humble themselves and ask for help. God had already shown me how difficult it was to admit I couldn't take care of myself. I admired these people for their willingness to accept our help, but actually I think they were the ones helping me.

My eating disorder made me extremely picky about what I would eat. I had lost all concept of what it means to be thankful for food. I saw food as the enemy. Sometimes I wished I would just never have to eat or think about food again. The people at the soup kitchen weren't given a long menu of fine cuisine to

"There have been periods of respite, but I only escape my overly self-critical thought life when passionate engagement distracts me."—Eva

"My focus is so often on what I look like and what I've eaten that I do not focus on Jesus and the work that he has for me and the ways I could be loving him and others. God has convicted me about how selfish my concern with how I look is, but it's so hard to stop thinking about these things. I am learning to believe that the Word of God is the true bread of life and that I need to feed myself spiritually as often as I'm thinking about physical food."—Mattie

Stepping Outside of Myself

choose from. They were mostly given other people's leftovers and donations. The food was plain, and the meat was not good quality. But they were thankful for it, and they treasured it. To them it meant life. I would never have dreamed of putting that food in my mouth. Seeing how these people appreciated the food they were given made me feel guilty for my attitude. I have been so blessed, far beyond anything I deserve. I can have virtually anything I want to eat at any time. Instead of coming to God with great thanks, I took his provisions for granted. I acted like an ungrateful and spoiled child.

Living on a college campus doesn't enable students to experience much of the real world. After arriving at the University of Virginia, I got settled in my comfortable college setting, and I rarely saw anyone except my fellow students. When I stepped out of my comfort zone, I saw that poverty and homelessness existed only a few minutes from my campus.

Living in that sheltered community made me lose perspective. My whole world revolved around me, my studies, my friends, and my tennis. I easily forgot that there's more to life than my daily activities. My self-absorption led me into a life of sin. I had developed a narrow, unhealthy view of life.

When I was struggling with my eating disorder, I thought I had more to deal with than I could handle. I thought life was so hard and unfair. In reality, I was letting the amount of fat and calories in the food I was eating make me miserable. I was tormented by my weight, while only five minutes from my house there were people who didn't know where their next meal would come from. In light of these people's problems, mine seemed so insignificant and ridiculous.

There are so many good reasons to be involved in outreach programs and to help the less fortunate. Not only do they desperately need help, but you also gain an amazing perspective by seeing how other people live. Taking my focus off myself at this time was exactly what I needed. Psalm 34:14 advises, "Turn from evil and do good." Giving my time and energy to help others helped me get a new perspective on life. God used that experience to make me more grateful for his blessings and to motivate me to continue on the road to healing.

Sharing My Story

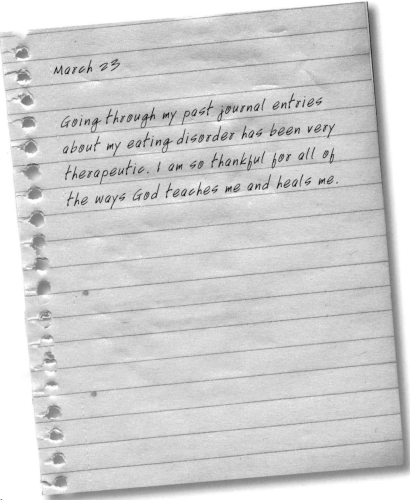

March 23

Going through my past journal entries about my eating disorder has been very therapeutic. I am so thankful for all of the ways God teaches me and heals me.

I was a junior in high school when I began to keep a daily journal. I started doing it as a part of my time with God each morning. At first my writing mostly consisted of my prayers. Once I developed the habit of journaling, my entries included more of my thoughts and emotions. When I first realized that my daily habit of journaling meant that I had unknowingly recorded the development of my eating disorder, I couldn't believe what a treasure I had. I had written down my thoughts about what I was experiencing throughout all my struggles. Going back through what I had written was extremely valuable. It helped me understand how and why this happened to me. My journal entries have been such an amazing blessing from God. They have enabled me to see all I have been through and how God has used this experience to shape who I am. In addition, writing this book and trying to explain what I was thinking at the time has helped

"I have learned to enjoy my exercise and my food. That is what I did differently earlier in high school that contributed to my overall happiness. I play tennis, walk more than I run, and lift lots of weights. I try not to eat when I am not hungry just so I don't get mad at myself for eating too much, and I try not to compare myself to those around me. I was never meant to be the skinny girl. God has so much more for me than just being thin."—Sophia

me tremendously. Having to express my thoughts and feelings forced me into a deeper understanding of what was going on in my life. The initial journaling helped me at the time, but further reflection on the experience gave me even greater clarity and perspective.

I have no doubt in my mind that everything happened to me for a reason and that God has a perfect plan for my life. If someone had told me at the beginning of college that I would have to go through all of this, I would have been frightened and probably angry, but the trials God put in front of me were for my own good. I will never again be the same person I was before my eating disorder. My heart will bear the scars of my experience with anorexia for the rest of my life, but I wouldn't trade those scars for anything.

In my youth group we used to sing a song called "Refiner's Fire." It describes the process of refining precious metals. Before being shaped into beautiful jewelry, gold or silver must be put into a fire to burn away the metal's impurities. Just like precious metal, I needed to be put into the fire so that God could purify my heart and make me into his precious servant. My eating disorder was my fire, and although it was the most difficult thing I have experienced, I know that God used it to refine me into the person he wants me to be. For that I will be forever grateful.

Who Am I?

The final phase in my journey through anorexia addresses the issue of rebuilding my identity. Identity development was at the heart of my eating disorder and recovery. Like many teenagers, I was wrestling with who I was and who I wanted to be. My experience with an eating disorder showed me that I had always based my identity on my performance—in school, in tennis, and in pleasing others. As I worked through these issues and came to understand the problems of having a performance-based mentality, I discovered the importance of rebuilding my identity in Christ alone. Although this entire story has been a journey of exploring my identity, these final pages more specifically address the question, Who am I?

Rebuilding My Identity

January 21, 2001

My recent work on my book motivated me to return to a counselor to talk about some of the residual effects of having an eating disorder. I have just returned from meeting with him, and I am so glad that I went. Our conversation was tremendously helpful to me. First he asked me to explain what was going on in my life now that had made me want to come in for a visit. I explained to him about my recent work on my book, as well as my preoccupation and dissatisfaction with my body. He helped me to realize that I do not have to let my anorexia define my identity. It was a period of my life that I went through as a result of the trauma that I experienced from leaving home, nothing more and nothing less.

Now it is good for me to be responsible about what I eat and how much I exercise. It is healthy for me to want to take care of myself. I trust myself more now to make my own judgments about what I should do. We talked about the subtle difference between being healthy and being anorexic. It made me realize that I know the difference between when I am trying to under-eat to wear away at my body and when I want to feel good because I have given my body the healthy kinds of foods that it wants.

We also talked about the possibility that my experience with anorexia may be an indication of some calling that I have in my life. Perhaps I am meant to be a writer and speaker on eating disorders and body image. I have pondered this question many times. But then we returned to the iden-tity issue. I do not want my bout with anorexia to define or consume who I am as a person. I am no longer anorexic, and I will not always have an eating disorder. This was a period of my life that was difficult, but I have many other dimensions that define who I am as a person.

At the end of our meeting, he told me that I could get in touch with him if I needed to talk some more, but he did not advise me to see another counselor. It was so liberating to be able to be honest with him about my feelings and for him not to recommend further counseling. I guess you could say he issued me a clean bill of health. I am hopeful now because I feel like I am finally free to have a healthy relationship with food and my body.

Finally, we also talked about having resolution to my problem, mourning it, and moving past it. I think that this project could be the last time that I write about anorexia. I will have said what I have wanted to say, and then I will be ready to move on in my career as a writer to do new things. Leaving college will bring a great deal of resolution to this stage in my life, as will completing this project. When I arrived home from the meeting, my books about anorexia had come in the mail, so it will be exciting to look through them and continue this journey of documenting my experiences. I now feel equipped to tackle what lies ahead in this project.

After fighting back from anorexia—changing my eating habits, becoming more comfortable with food, and becoming less obsessive about my exercise—there was one final, lingering effect of my eating disorder. The area of my life that was still in the shadow of my anorexia was my body image and self-worth. After gaining almost twenty pounds from my lightest weight, I was haunted by a continual sense of feeling fat. Although I wasn't by any means overweight, I just felt so much bigger than I had been. At times I hated my body, and

I was constantly looking in the mirror to see whether or not I was fat. Ultimately, I knew that my insecurities about my body stemmed from misplaced self-worth. After correcting the other self-destructive aspects of my eating disorder, I was not going to let myself continue to be dominated by a negative body image. I would still be satisfied with nothing less than a complete recovery. I sensed that this was my final hurdle.

In the midst of my anorexia I defined myself by the world's standards. Like many other women, I looked for value in my physical form. Self-worth is one of the most challenging aspects of life for most women today. Proverbs 31 provides a rich description of the virtuous woman. In my search for a positive sense of self-worth, I looked to the woman depicted in these verses. Verses 29–30 read, "'Many women do noble things, but you surpass them all.' Charm is deceptive, and beauty is fleeting; but a woman who fears the

"Through these struggles, I have been able to cling to God for confidence and peace. I think I will always battle these struggles to a certain extent, but God has put my heart at rest. I have learned what it truly means to lay things at his feet and leave them there. He has shown me that he made me as his perfect creation, and he desires for me to honor him through taking care of my body. He has blessed me with people in my life that continue to affirm me and encourage me to have a positive body image."—Andrea

"I got my worth from the scale. It finally helped to know that in God's eyes I was accepted and worthy. I was perfect."—Krista

Rebuilding My Identity

LORD is to be praised." I had certainly not been living as if I believed beauty is fleeting. I was beginning to see that my true worth would be found in my love for God, my faith in God, and my fear of God. These qualities were far more important than my clothing size could ever be.

One of the most valuable things I did to redefine my sense of self-worth was to spend time in God's Word. I read passages such as these from Psalm 139: "I praise you because I am fearfully and wonderfully made" (v. 14) and "Search me, O God, and know my heart; test me and know my anxious thoughts. See if there is any offensive way in me, and lead me in the way everlasting" (vv. 23–24). I memorized verses, read God's promises about my identity, and retrained myself to trust that my self-worth was in Christ. Gradually, I could feel God setting me free from the burden of my negative body image.

During this time I also discovered that how I felt about myself was a choice. I could choose to define my worth based on what I looked like, what I did, and what others thought of me, or I could choose to define myself by my identity in Christ. Just as I could choose to be insecure about my body, I could also choose to live confidently in the love of Christ.

There was a time before my eating disorder when I didn't base my self-worth on my weight. I knew that since I had lived like that before, there must be some way I could find my way back and recover my sense of identity. If I could remember who I was before my anorexia, I could let go of my need to define myself by my weight. I wasn't willing to resign myself to this slavery. As Galatians 5:1 says, "It is for freedom that Christ has set us free. Stand firm, then, and do not let yourselves be burdened again by a yoke of slavery." I had to stand firm and fight for an identity apart from my weight.

Having a negative body image was my way of holding on to my eating disorder. I couldn't put what I had been through behind me until I let go of this last remaining effect. I knew I had to let go of it all to find freedom. Lisa Bevere writes, "Let go of your past because your past is not your future. . . . Now is the time to put the past to rest" (76–77). Now that I had wrestled with everything I had been through, I knew it was time to let go of my anorexia and move on. Anorexia had already claimed too much of my life. As I put my past behind me now and I move ahead, I don't know what the future holds for me, but I am able to trust that God will faithfully provide for me as he has throughout all of these experiences.

Dear Lord, thank you for the experience of my anorexia. Thank you for how you used this to shape me into the servant that you want me to be. I pray that you would continue to work on my heart and that I would be open to whatever you would have to teach me. I pray also for all of the women who struggle with these issues as I have. I pray that you would give us the strength to fight against the world's standards and to realize that our identity—our truest sense of self-worth—comes from your love for us through Christ. Amen.

Your Story

Thank you for journeying through this story with me. I hope that it has been both challenging and encouraging to you. As I conclude, I want to leave you with one final challenge.

Eating, exercise, and body image have become hot topics in our culture today. Many people are controlled by overeating, undereating, overexercising, underexercising, being obsessed with their bodies, and having a negative body image. As a result, this is an area of our lives where we can set ourselves apart as Christians.

Just as you may go to church on Sundays or avoid alcohol, drugs, or sex as a way of demonstrating that you are a Christian, resist the cultural temptation to give in to a negative body image and an unhealthy relationship with food and exercise. This is an opportunity for us to demonstrate to those around us what it means to have a strong identity built on Christ and not a sense of self-worth that is based on performance or other people's opinions of us. Believe it or not, you can be a witness to what God has done in your life simply by how you relate to food, exercise, and your body.

You might be wondering how to go about making this sort of change in your life. While it is certainly an ongoing process, let me give you a place to start. In the final pages you will find an outline called "Who Am I? Building Identity in Christ." Each characteristic is followed by Scripture verses that you can look up. Reading through God's Word and reprogramming my idea of who I was, based on his truth, was a turning point in my life. I encourage you to use this resource to discover who God has created you to be.

I challenge you to be different, to be secure in your relationship with God—secure enough that you can appreciate the body that he has created for you, that you can enjoy the food that he abundantly provides for you, and that you can rejoice in an active lifestyle that brings glory to God.

Who Am I?
Building Identity in Christ

I am accepted and worthy.	Ps. 139:13–18; Rom. 15:7
I am competent.	2 Cor. 3:5–6; Phil. 4:13
I am free from fear.	2 Tim. 1:7; 1 Peter 5:7
I am strong.	Ps. 37:39; Dan. 11:32; Phil. 4:19
I have wisdom.	Prov. 2:6–7; 1 Cor. 1:30; James 1:5
I am free from guilt.	John 8:36
I am perfectly loved.	John 15:9; Rom. 8:35–39; Eph. 2:4–5
I have the mind of Christ.	1 Cor. 2:16
I have hope.	Pss. 16:11; 27:13; 31:24; Rom. 15:4, 13
I am an adopted child of God.	Rom. 8:16–17; Gal. 4:4–7
I am totally forgiven.	Ps. 103:12; Col. 1:13–14; 2:13
I have been chosen.	Eph. 1:4
I am seen as perfect.	Heb. 10:14
I lack nothing.	Phil. 4:19
I have been declared righteous.	Rom. 3:24; 1 Cor. 1:30
I am victorious.	Rom. 8:37; 2 Cor. 2:14; 1 John 5:3–4

I have God's power.	Acts 1:7–8; Eph. 3:16–18
I am never alone.	Deut. 31:6; Rom. 8:38–39
I am protected.	Ps. 32:7
I have authority over Satan.	Col. 1:13; 1 John 4:4
I have confidence.	Prov. 3:26; Eph. 3:12; Heb. 10:19
I have security.	Prov. 14:26
I am blameless.	John 3:18; Rom. 8:1–2
I have been created for good works.	Eph. 2:10
I have freedom.	Ps. 32:7; 2 Cor. 2:14
I have comfort.	John 16:7; 2 Cor. 1:3–4
I am made pure.	1 John 3:3
I am a friend of Christ.	John 15:14–15
I am a temple of the Holy Spirit.	1 Cor. 3:16; 6:19
I can come before God.	Eph. 2:18
I am a new creation.	2 Cor. 5:17
I am born of God.	1 John 5:18
I am dead to sin.	Rom. 6:6, 11
I can obtain grace in times of need.	Heb. 4:16
I cannot be separated from God.	Rom. 8:31–39
I can overcome the world.	1 John 5:4–5
I am alive with Christ.	Gal. 2:20; Eph. 2:5
I am not anxious.	Phil. 4:6
I am renewed.	2 Cor. 4:16
I am being refined.	1 Peter 1:6–7
I am known.	2 Tim. 2:19

Adapted from Sylvia Gunter, *Who I Am in Christ* (1991)

Resources

National Eating Disorders Association (NEDA)
800-931-2237
www.nationaleatingdisorders.org

National Association of Anorexia Nervosa and Associated
Disorders (ANAD)
847-831-3438
www.anad.org

Eating Disorders Information Network (EDIN)
404-816-3346
www.edin-ga.org

Anorexia Nervosa and Related Eating Disorders, Inc.
(ANRED)
www.anred.com

The National Eating Disorder Information Centre (of Canada)
1-866-NEDIC-20 or (in Toronto) 416-340-4156
www.nedic.ca

Bibliography

American Psychiatric Association (APA). *Diagnostic and Statistical Manual of Mental Disorders*. 4th ed. Washington, DC: APA, 1994.

Bevere, Lisa. *The True Measure of a Woman: You Are More Than What You See*. Lake Mary, FL: Creation House, 1997.

Bondi, Roberta C. *Memories of God: Theological Reflections on Life*. Nashville: Abingdon, 1995.

Brumberg, Joan Jacobs. *The Body Project: An Intimate History of American Girls*. New York: Vintage, 1997.

_____. *Fasting Girls: The History of Anorexia Nervosa*. New York: Vintage, 2000.

Colson, Charles C. *Born Again*. Grand Rapids: Revell, 2000.

Hornbacher, Marya. *Wasted: A Memoir of Anorexia and Bulimia*. New York: Harper Perennial, 1998.

Normandi, C. E., and L. Roark. *It's Not about Food*. New York: Perigee, 1998.

Pipher, Mary. *Reviving Ophelia*. New York: Ballantine, 1994.

Christie Pettit, a native of Houston, attended the University of Virginia as a scholarship athlete on the varsity women's tennis team, majoring in psychology and religious studies. Christie received a master of theological studies at Emory University's Candler School of Theology, where she continued to focus on the relationship between the body and spirituality. Christie then went on to earn a master of marriage and family therapy from the Psychological Studies Institute and now works with teenage girls and young adult women as a counselor at the Hope Counseling Center. She also serves as the managing editor for *Conversations: A Forum for Authentic Transformation*. Christie lives with her husband, Peter, in Atlanta.

Ditch **MEAN** for good
with help from Hayley!

Available at your local bookstore

If what you're showing ain't on the menu, keep it covered up!

SEXYGIRLS

How Hot Is Too Hot?

HAYLEY DiMARCO

BEST-SELLING AUTHOR OF *MEAN GIRLS* AND *DATEABLE*

Available at your local bookstore